ENTREPRENEUR REVOLUTION

THIRD EDITION

ENTREPRENEUR REVOLUTION

THIRD EDITION

HOW TO DEVELOP YOUR ENTREPRENEURIAL MINDSET AND START A BUSINESS THAT WORKS

DANIEL PRIESTLEY

CAPSTONE
A Wiley Brand

Library of Congress Cataloging-in-Publication Data is Available:

ISBN 9780857089731 (Paperback)
ISBN 9780857089748 (ePub)
ISBN 9780857089755 (ePDF)

Cover Design: Wiley
Cover Images: © nadiinko/Adobe Stock Photos; © warmworld/ Adobe Stock Photos

Set in 11/16pt and Adobe Jenson Pro by Straive, Chennai, India.

SKY10070008_031924

DEDICATION

This book is dedicated to the bravest, most authentic, creative, expansive, dynamic people I know: the entrepreneurs of the world.

To the farmer I met in Uganda who had the courage to take a micro-loan and lift herself from poverty through her chicken business.

To the IT manager who dared to pitch an 'impossible idea' to the chairman of his bank and created three iconic businesses, and has helped hundreds of entrepreneurs and became the best mentor I could have dreamed of.

To the 16-year-old who started Student magazine and ended up inspiring a generation of entrepreneurs.

To the 30-year-old who was fired from his own technology company for being too disruptive, only to save the company ten years later by revolutionising every industry he touched. True icons leave early – we will miss him.

To the person who bit the bullet today and registered their first business.

This book is my tribute to you. I'm just as excited as you are!

CONTENTS

INTRODUCTION

We are living through revolutionary times. The rules that created commercial success in the past have radically changed. Doing what worked yesterday will not bring you success tomorrow.

For some people, this will be a time of great uncertainty and loss. For others it will be the greatest opportunity in history. The conditions are perfect for almost anyone in the world to create a successful business that completely changes their life for the better.

An entrepreneur is simply someone who spots an opportunity and acts to make it into a commercial success.

This book is written to help you to become better at spotting opportunities and turning them into a commercial success.

A revolution is a great shift in society, where an old system is thrown out and a new one is embraced. In all of history, the real fortunes are made in revolutionary times. The difference with this revolution is that it presents a chance for wealth to spread to a lot more people. The tools, technology and opportunities that have shown up recently are designed to empower people. Lots of people.

Today, farmers in rural India have access to more information and computing power than NASA had when it launched the Voyager missions.

Today, a teenager in their bedroom has more tools for building a global enterprise than Coca-Cola did when it grew internationally.

A small business based in London can easily have a tech developer in Uzbekistan, a customer service representative in the Philippines, an accountant in India and a sales person in South Africa. This little team might talk to each other every day but have never met up in person. Despite having no offices or factories, they might have thousands of customers across several countries.

Today, your business ideas have more potential to become massively successful than ever before in history.

For whatever reason, you were born to live through these exciting times. You weren't born to live in the dark ages as a serf, you weren't born to live in the agricultural ages as a farmer, you weren't born to live in the industrial age as a factory worker. You are alive during a unique point in history; a time where anything is possible for you.

This book is here to wake up the part of you that can spot opportunities and make them successful. Not just any opportunities, but those that are right for you.

In these pages you will discover that there's a part of your brain that is already highly entrepreneurial and wants to build something you can be proud of. You'll discover exactly how to live in the 'entrepreneur sweet spot,' where you do what you love, you do something of value and you get rewarded generously for it.

This book will challenge you too. I've laid out ten challenges for you to get started on almost immediately. They are designed to push your buttons and get you out of your comfort zone.

We will explore a high-performance mindset and culture, so that no matter how many complex decisions you face, you will always find a way to move forward.

I'm going to share with you the keys to creating a product ecosystem that scales up to make more money than you've ever made – hopefully by orders of magnitude. I'll also share the code I've used to create small, high-performing teams that achieve more than companies with 10× bigger headcounts.

Best of all, we will do this in a way that is fun, adventurous and makes a positive impact. I want you to love the process of becoming a great entrepreneur, not just the results you get.

YOU MIGHT WANT TO READ THIS BOOK MORE THAN ONCE

I've hidden gems in this book – ideas that have taken me decades to figure out and codify. On every page you'll hopefully find a sentence that sparks an idea or challenges you to do something differently. Rather than rushing through the book and then getting stuck into the next one, focus on implementation. When a brainwave hits you, stop reading. Make notes, fire off an email to action what you've learned or make a call to discuss your plans with a friend.

Many people have said to me that they got more from this book the second time they read it. In particular I'd like this book to reveal to you something hidden.

There's an underlying theme, relating to a key ingredient, that you need if you really want to be successful. You might spot it straight away, or it might come to you later.

If you do spot the new ingredient, pay particular attention to put it into everything you do. This new ingredient hasn't been necessary in business up until this point but, from now on, it must be at the very heart of what you do.

I'm going to mention this ingredient many times in the book, but I won't say what it is specifically for you. I will leave you to find it.

When you read through this book, look for this magic ingredient, or at least look for clues. If something in these pages really makes your emotions flow or your head buzz, it's probably an indication of what this ingredient might be.

The beginning is important and the end will unfold but, at the centre, you might discover a mountain of value you never noticed when you first looked.

Sometimes people read this book and 'get it' right away. Some people get it on the second or third read. I've not hidden this key ingredient from you; if anything it's actually right under your nose.

Whatever you do, don't stop looking. You simply can't build a successful enterprise without this ingredient in the Entrepreneur Revolution.

Good luck. I hope you love reading this book.

To see videos of these and other case studies visit: www.dent.global/entrev

CHAPTER 1

THE ENTREPRENEUR REVOLUTION IS UNFOLDING

You live at the most incredible time in history. A massive transfer of wealth, power and possibility is taking place. If you approach it with the right mindset and strategy you will make a fortune by pursuing your passion and you will solve meaningful problems and improve the world along the way.

What's taking place is a revolution. Everything as you know it is changing and in the coming years the pace of change will accelerate.

The nature of work, lifestyle and wealth is all radically shifting in real time.

Before we look forward, however, let's look backwards at the last revolution.

Let's begin at the agricultural age. If you went back to 1750 in a time machine, the chances are the first person you would meet would be a farmer. The agricultural age was defined by the fact that most people worked the land.

Then came a series of technological breakthroughs. The steam engine, fossil fuels and machinery.

One tractor could do the work of 100 men in the field. One textile factory could make all the suits for a city at a fraction of the cost of a tailor. More energy could be extracted from lumps of coal than we could harness from our most impressive horses.

The technology changed things. You couldn't fight it, you couldn't avoid it, it was a revolution. The nature of work, life, education, healthcare and wealth creation massively transformed.

If you took your time machine back any time between about 1850 and the year 2000, there's a lot less chance you would meet a single farmer, even if you tried. You would meet factory workers.

In the early part of the revolution, you would see people who worked on machines making products. They were 'blue-collar' factory workers. If you went back to the late 1900s you would find people working on the new machines – computers – making data. These were 'white-collar' factory workers.

Regardless of the colour of their collar, their labour is repetitive. They sit at their work station and they repeat their tasks for hours on end until the day is over. This is just how it is for most people who live in the industrial age.

We have left the Industrial Revolution and we are now entering a new era. We are seeing the way people live and work dramatically shifting again. In this book we will call this new era the 'Entrepreneur Revolution'.

If you took your time machine forward to any time in the next 100 years you would most likely meet people whose work is very entrepreneurial. They probably don't work in a traditional office alongside hundreds of other similar workers. A lot of their work might look like play; their days might involve creating media to connect with a global audience, attending online workshops, creating something valuable with a coworker in a distant city or collaborating with an artificial intelligence (AI) system to make improvements to a campaign.

Most people will work in very entrepreneurial ways with entrepreneurial teams. Rather than having a traditional job at a massive company and receiving a monthly salary, they will be working in smaller more dynamic team and will probably earn money based on performance or part ownership of the firm.

Once again, it's technology that has changed things. A series of recent breakthroughs has robbed the big factories of their awesome competitive advantage and given an edge to small businesses.

Technology has made it possible for any small businesses to have a big impact. Today a tiny business can easily find clients globally, access factories or tech developers, create media and be open for business 24/7.

Small businesses can do almost all the things big businesses can do; and they can do something more.

A small business has spirit. It has a team of people who care, they know their customers, they love what they do, they respond faster, there's less red tape, the workplace is more fun and everyone gets to have a say.

Your future is going to look very different to what your parents probably imagined it would be.

TECHNOLOGY HAS SET THE SCENE

When a company has less than 150 staff, everyone tends to know everyone else. There's a buzz and an excitement. There's a tribal feeling that often gets lost in big corporations.

When the founder of the business is involved in its operations, there's magic. Rarely is this magic scalable for big business.

For these reasons and more, top performers are going to quit their jobs and start businesses. They are going to take with them other top performers.

These entrepreneurial teams will be faster, more cost effective, more nimble, more responsive and more profitable.

If technology has created a revolution, let's take a quick look at how this revolution got started and what's likely to happen in the coming years.

In the late 1800s the telephone was invented, but it wasn't until the 1920s that it took off. It made it feasible for businesses to have multiple local locations.

In the 1920s commercial air travel was born, but it wasn't until the 1950s that it was popularised. Once again, there was a 20–30 year lag time before the systemic changes arrived. Once air travel was widely available, we saw the birth of national and international companies.

In the 1930s, along came television. However, most people believe it was a 1950s phenomenon – again, a 20-year lag time. Television gave birth to the brand. Whoever dominated the airwaves dominated people's spending habits.

Jump forward to the late 1960s and you will see the first computers. It wasn't until the 1980s, however, that computers were being purchased by a significant number of businesses or individuals.

You might not have spotted it right away but, if you looked closely, in the 1980s and 1990s people were beginning to use their computers in home-based business.

These home-based businesses might have been tiny, but they didn't necessarily appear so. For the first time in over 100 years, small businesses could be just as competitive as large businesses in a few industries.

In 1989, Tim Berners-Lee came up with the World Wide Web and the Internet was born. Again, it took close to decades for the majority to adopt it.

In 1998, Google made the whole web searchable. Anything you want, anyone you need, any question you have, all discovered in a matter of seconds. This gave rise to businesses that could offer highly niche products and services that would previously never have found a market.

In 2004, social media was born, democratising information in a way that enabled people who shared common interests to find each other and share ideas as never before. A couple of decades later and social media has displaced all forms of traditional media and every person consumes a totally unique diet of media alongside a community of people who are similar in values but not in geography.

Apple launched the iPhone in 2007 and began the process of putting a supercomputer in everyone's pocket. The impact was far from instantaneous though. A decade later, the true impact of these smartphones was only beginning to be understood.

In 2008, cloud computing was born, giving rise to the 'virtual business'. Staff and customers can be anywhere in the world and the business is exactly the same. Work can be done from home, teams can be spaced out globally and no one cares.

More recently, the explosive introduction of generative AI hit the mainstream and in 2023 over 100 million people started using ChatGPT. AI will totally disrupt and reshape every aspect of the way we live and work in the years to come.

Don't forget, though, that there's a significant lag time for business to catch on to a trend and reorganise the way things operate. Looking back, we see that it often takes over 10 years for even a massive trend to make a splash and reveal the true nature of the impact it makes on society.

We don't need to wait though; we know what's going to happen.

All of this technology allows a small business to look big. It makes micro-niches accessible. It levels the global playing field.

THE NEW WORLD OF WORK

Where would you rather work if given the choice? Would you like to work in a large, soulless company that cares only about its balance sheet and treats you like a number? Or, instead, would you like to be part of a small, dynamic team of creative people who are servicing the needs of a niche you feel passionate about?

Most people are in the process of evaluating their options and have noticed big corporate is no longer what it used to be and small business isn't so small anymore. Many people are being forcibly displaced from their traditional jobs and find themselves cast into the entrepreneurial world, having to make changes in order to survive.

As a result of technology changes the world of work has changed and huge numbers of people globally will either start a business or join an entrepreneurial team. These people are no longer in the industrial system, they are part of the Entrepreneur Revolution.

Entrepreneurship is about the team, not about the founder of the business. In my opinion, founders get too much credit. Entrepreneurship is about taking a risk to make valuable things happen.

In that context, high-performing entrepreneurial teams can only exist because the 'entrepreneurship' is shared by a group of collaborators and not just the person who started the business entity on day one.

Taking your place in the Entrepreneur Revolution requires that you create value, to take on meaningful work and to care deeply about what you are involved in. You'll be fulfilling the desires of others and getting paid for the results you create rather than the time you clock in for. Whether you start the business or join a dynamic band of rebels, you'll be part of this mega trend and you'll be expected to think different.

Chances are, if you are a top performer, you want to work somewhere that you are recognised and where you feel that the work you do makes a difference. You also want to either own a piece of the business you work for or get paid in line with the value you create.

If you're entrepreneurial, this is your time. Never in history has there been a better moment for you to start or grow a business that brings excitement to the workplace and makes an inspiring difference to the world. There's never been more opportunities to make massive amounts of money – in exciting and fun ways.

The Entrepreneur Revolution is taking place. There's no point fighting it. It's happening.

The rest of this book is designed to help you to transition out of the old and into the new. It's designed to get you ahead of the curve, seeing the future and making the most of it.

Just like the farmers had to change the way they viewed the world or they would end up as factory fodder, we too must change. We must develop a more entrepreneurial nature.

We must awaken the part of us that loves change and challenges. The part of us that takes responsibility for outcomes and that cares deeply about others. The part of us that sees opportunities and knows how to seize them.

We must cease being industrial age workers and start being entrepreneurs.

LET'S LOOK AT THE SYSTEM

When I look around, I see plenty of people still living according to a system that makes very little sense to me anymore.

I see people giving up the best part of their day, to push power to a corporation that doesn't inspire them, for a small amount of money that barely affords them a comfortable life.

I see people stuck with mortgages that limit every decision they make. People who stay living in towns because they grew up there but who no longer find fulfilment there.

I notice some people spend time with friends they don't respect or admire. They are friends just because they have always been friends.

I see people who hold on to ideas that don't really make a lot of sense to them but they believe because everyone else does.

So many people are living by their past decisions. Or, even worse, they are living by someone else's past decisions.

Over the last 150 years that hasn't been such a bad thing. The Industrial Revolution set the tone; working for a factory or a big corporation was the norm. As a worker you needed to be on site every day from 9am to 5pm, holidays had to be squeezed into your annual leave, fun was something you could look forward to when you were too old for it. But there weren't any alternatives.

Everyone alive today has new powers to create from anywhere in the world. You don't need any permission to set up the modern equivalent of a TV station, newspaper or radio programme and it's for free. The Internet takes your ideas and products and distributes them for you globally. It allows you to make big money from tiny, silly little ideas that you care about.

Radically, we can make money from our passion. This is an idea that seems so foreign to so many. For eons, work was work for the masses. The concept of pursuing a passion might have been reserved for nobility at best.

In this new digital economy, you are free to earn while you explore. Your personal breakthroughs, journey of self-discovery and creativity replaces the daily grind of the traditional workplace.

At the beginning of the Industrial Revolution a factory cost a fortune to set up. Now the means of production cost a few thousand dollars to set up. To be in business today requires you to have a phone and an idea.

This has given birth to a new breed of person: part owner, part worker, part artist. The new breed of workers are taking over – entrepreneurs.

MY STORY

For me, this has been a discovery I have witnessed first-hand.

I am an entrepreneur. I grew up in a beachside town in Australia. As a teenager I worked at McDonald's, I delivered pizza, I went door-to-door selling and I worked behind a bar but all I wanted to be was an entrepreneur. I read books about business, I read business magazines and I collected articles about entrepreneurs who had been successful.

At 18, I went to university to study business. I believed that I would be rubbing shoulders with multimillionaire entrepreneurs and learning about how to raise big money, grow fast and exit big.

I was disappointed at university. None of my lecturers had built or sold businesses. Most of them were struggling and wanted boring jobs.

At age 19, I dropped out of university to work directly for a successful entrepreneur. I shadowed him for almost two years. I learned all about sales, marketing, product creation, team building and managing fast growth. It was exactly the kind of learning I had wanted from university!

I founded my first company at 21 years old after two years of apprenticeship in a fast-growth marketing business.

I created a highly niched marketing business specializing in event marketing and sales follow-up. By 25, I had a team of over 15 people and we were generating millions in sales.

At 25, I decided to expand internationally and set up an office in London. We generated millions in sales in the first year despite being warned that London was a tough city.

In my late 20s, business took me all over the world. I visited dozens of countries, did deals, worked alongside some awe-inspiring entrepreneurs and rubbed shoulders with my childhood heroes.

At age 29, I wrote a book called *Key Person of Influence*. It became a business best-seller and it put me in contact with thousands of entrepreneurs.

As a result, we set up Dent Global, a business growth accelerator specialising in small service businesses. Within three years we were set up in multiple countries, helping hundreds of entrepreneurs to grow their businesses with support from some of the world's most successful business leaders who are part of the programme.

In the 2010s, I bought up a group of businesses and grew them. The group included Rethink Press, a niche publishing business that has become the UK's top producer of non-fiction books. I bought and sold Ecademy .com, a social network with over 500,000 members. It included SOTechnology, which was sold to a publicly listed AI company in the USA, as well as August Recognition, a niche agency focused on entering and winning quality awards.

In 2020, I co-founded a software business, Score-App, which has grown to become the global leader for quiz marketing and pioneered AI-generated quizzes and data analytics for small businesses. In 2023, I co-founded BookMagic.ai, a software platform that allows authors to write and publish a book with the support of AI tools.

I live the Entrepreneur Revolution lifestyle. I can travel the world while working, I earn money from global small businesses, my time is my own, I raise money for causes that matter to me and I feel a huge sense of freedom.

When I want to take a break I can; when I want to attend an exciting event I do; if I want to buy something, I don't often need to think about the money.

Better still, almost every day I get emails from clients saying they love working with us, they want to recommend us and they feel we've made a difference to them.

It's a foreign idea to wake up to an alarm, to have a person who I think of as my boss, or to ask permission to take a holiday.

I have an awesome team. My business partners are my closest friends, we have incredibly talented people who have been proudly creating with us for years. We have charity partners who are now expanding their reach as a result of the partnership we have with them.

I'm not saying all that to be boastful, I'm saying it because I feel it has come as a result of the Entrepreneur Revolution. I owe my lifestyle to the new emerging world. I owe my lifestyle to the availability of key technologies. I owe it to the Internet being everywhere, valuable digital services being cheap or free, the cloud making my enterprise instantly global and living in an age of collaboration.

There's absolutely nothing special about me. I don't have any special skills or record-breaking intelligence. I use technology to build teams, create things people want and build communities of customers. The only thing that is unique about me is I have an entrepreneurial mindset.

Most people still have a mindset that was crafted by the Industrial Revolution school system. In the same way that your computer can't function properly without upgrading its software, you must also be willing to delete some old files from your mind and install some new ideas so you can see opportunities and succeed at them.

A System that No Longer Makes Sense

The Industrial Revolution was an awe-inspiring time in history. However, it's a system that no longer serves you. The system is made up of rules and ideas that were perfect for the Industrial Revolution but they are no longer right for people who choose to live in the Entrepreneur Revolution.

The Industrial Revolution needed workers to perform meaningless, repetitive tasks. It needed lots of them. The Industrial Revolution created schools and institutions designed to reinforce this way of living.

The Entrepreneur Revolution needs people who are passionate, free thinking, inspired innovators. The systems and rules you were taught at school are not a good fit for producing the types of people who thrive today.

Let's take a look at three common ideas – ideas that worked for the Industrial Revolution but don't serve you in the Entrepreneur Revolution:

1. 'Work hard now and you will get your rewards later.'
2. 'Work isn't meant to be fun.'
3. 'Work hard to prove how smart you are.'

These are just three examples to show how differently you must start to think if you're going to take full advantage of the times we are in.

Let's start with dismantling the first idea.

OLD IDEA: WORK HARD NOW AND YOU WILL GET YOUR REWARDS LATER

This idea is in religion, in institutional work, in governments, in schools and many other places you look – the idea that you should make sacrifices now for some far-off reward in the future.

It isn't the case. Right here, in this moment, is all your power, all your joy, all your life force. You have no power in the future or in the past, it's all here in this moment.

When you are present, you make better choices and you spot great opportunities all around you. When you project yourself into the future or the past you lose your power.

The Entrepreneur Revolution is about pursuing a path you enjoy being on with people you love spending time with.

When you are following an inspired path the rewards are in the present moment and will compound to create even bigger rewards in the future as well.

People who are paralysed by the 'jam tomorrow game', are stuck doing something they hate because they think some day it will pay off and the rewards will be worth it. They lose their spark, they project their power into a distant future and they miss opportunities to succeed now. The dull path is terrible now and it gets worse the longer you stay on it.

Agents of the Industrial Revolution controlled workers with the idea that in the future they would have great rewards for their labour if they suffered now. People had no choice but to put their dreams on hold to do monotonous work. They needed a fantasy of retirement to counterweight the workload they were enduring.

Today if you're doing something you hate, the sacrifice probably won't deliver a pay-off in the future. You will probably just spend a whole lifetime making sacrifices and then get resentful that you're too old to do the things that really matter to you.

If you continue to sacrifice, you will probably realise after it's too late that a great life is made up of great days.

NEW IDEA: THERE IS NO PAY DAY, THERE'S JUST LIFE

In the age of endless technologies and connectivity, if your work is boring, relative or hard, someone has already figured out how to automate it or outsource it to another lower cost country. It's only a matter of time before you'll be displaced – contrary to the plan, your hard work will bring even more pain.

A more fruitful way to live in this era is as if you will never retire. The goal is to work in a way that the idea of retiring is not exciting or desirable. Imagine what you would do for work if you knew you would have to do it until you drop. Imagine a way of working that involves travelling, sharing ideas, creating campaigns, supporting causes and having time for creative freedom and learning about topics that interest you. Imagine getting paid top-tier income to have fun.

Reading this, you might start to feel annoyed. You might think that sacrificing now for a distant reward is just the way it is and that I am mad for suggesting otherwise.

Playing the 'delayed gratification game' by putting joyful things off for the future, might have worked for people in the past but this is now. It's highly unlikely that retirement systems will be sustainable in the coming years; with an ageing population governments and companies are going to wiggle their way out of most obligations just to stay solvent.

When I speak to people who are diligently playing the delayed gratification game, it typically hasn't yielded much for them or if it has, the sacrifice wasn't worth it. They gave up the best part of their 20s and 30s only to spark a reckless midlife crisis later in life.

When I probe into a person's best choice, more often than not it arose from being brave and seizing the moment. Rarely do people achieve momentous things because they hesitated and put off what their heart was calling them to do.

For me the idea of passing up the most energetic years of my life so I can take a few Euro-getaway tours in my 70s is a non-starter. Why play golf when you could have played anything? Why wait until you are too old to do the things you are waiting to do?

Why cash in the nest egg when you could have been free as a bird in the first place?

One reason is fear. We are scared of living in the present and having more enjoyment now because of what might happen in the future. The Industrial Revolution mindset convinces people that joy is something limited and needs to be rationed. Ironically, from a centred place, here in the present, we have our most authentic and powerful visions for the future.

The place to plan your future is in the present. The best place is on the beach or in a forest or in a rooftop penthouse apartment. If you are inspired you will create an inspired vision. If you are fearful you will create a vision based on mitigating your fear. It will be about scarcity and not abundance.

I'm not saying that you don't have goals, dreams and plans. I'm saying that you are living in a time where they can happen now, not later. You can enjoy the journey as much as the destination.

Old Idea: Work Isn't Meant to be Fun

My grandfather worked hard. He was a factory technician making copper cable. It was hard work, in hot tin sheds with loud machines.

My grandfather got injured at work. He almost blinded himself when sparks flew in his face. Another time he chopped off a big chunk of his finger when he was operating heavy machinery. He didn't take time off, he was back at work the next day.

Apparently this was a good thing. It proved how hard he was willing to work and that getting work done was most important.

He got promoted to a junior manager, a foreman, then a middle manager. Eventually he became the general manager of the whole factory.

He never expected that work would be fun, he had his weekends for that. On weekends he liked to play golf or go fishing. Golf and fishing were fun, work was hard. Simple.

Many of us are stuck with these remnants of the industrialised worker mentality. We think it's wrong to have fun all day, it's wasteful to sit and daydream, it's bad to question authority. There's only one thing you are allowed to do without guilt – work – and the less fun it is the better.

NEW IDEA: FUN BUILDS YOUR BUSINESS

In the Entrepreneur Revolution it doesn't have to be that way. If my grandfather was alive today, and so inclined, he could easily make golf and fishing his business. He could build a website, he could invent products, he could have a community of like-minded people who subscribe to his tips, he could be an affiliate for other great products that he discovers.

Today, he could join a team anywhere in the world and work from home. His passion, combined with his methodical approach, could make him invaluable to a global small business.

Today, working hard probably indicates you are doing something functional, not something valuable. The value of anything functional is trending towards zero.

People who thrive in the Entrepreneur Revolution don't work hard. They create, they get stuff done, they make things happen, they organise change, they drive projects, they engineer results and energise teams.

Sometimes this requires dedicated effort, sometimes it takes time to work the angles, often there's many conversations to be had. However, it's not 'work' that is being done. At least not in the traditional sense. A great game has its challenges and requires effort but it's fun.

Old Idea: Work Hard to Prove how Smart You are

One of the first rules you learn in school is that it's wrong to look to others for answers. If you pay a smart kid to do your maths homework, you're a cheat. If you find someone who's done the work before and use it, you're a cheat. If you have answers to problems and you sell them to others, you're a cheat.

Why on earth is all that called cheating? These are valuable skills as an entrepreneur. True entrepreneurs don't try to do their own homework, they find the best people they can afford to do it for them.

In school, if you see your friend has come up with a great answer to a problem, and you then copy it or improve upon it, you are labelled a copycat.

The kid who 'improved upon a competitor's best practices' gets punished and nothing happens to the kid who left his 'intellectual property unprotected'.

We should punish the child who created valuable answers but carelessly left them to be discovered by the competition. That would more accurately reflect the real world today.

The goal of the Industrial Revelation school system was to turn high-spirited little kids into reliable 'component labour' – a component is something that will fit nicely into a bigger machine – and that was their vision for what successful humans should be like.

Big businesses or organisations were machines and they needed replacement parts. The school system was tasked with creating those rigid, uniformed little cogs that would slot right in. The entrepreneur revolution doesn't value those cogs very much anymore.

NEW IDEA: SMART PEOPLE SURROUND THEMSELVES WITH SMARTER PEOPLE

The Entrepreneur Revolution requires you to have energy and to pass that energy on to others. Rather than being a cog, you need to be more like a node.

A node inside a computer becomes more valuable if it is well connected to millions of other nodes. It contains information and passes that information on. Energy flows through the node and the more energy and information it can pass on to the network, the more valuable it is.

Being smart in business is about finding the best people to work with you. You don't show how smart you are by having every answer; you show how smart you are by having fast access to every answer.

In business we reward the person who can find the answers quickly and who can use them to innovate in a new way.

Great entrepreneurs turn ideas into teams and those teams rapidly produce products, marketing campaigns, sales and profit. A truly great entrepreneur is not the most skilful and knowledgeable person on their team – not even close. They are the person who has attracted the most brilliant people around them.

Today, the schooling system should find ways to reward students who can successfully form a team and solve the entire year's worth of homework in a few weeks while having a great time together.

If you went to school, you are probably riddled with old ideas that don't serve you in the new times we're entering. In the next chapter we will expose some more of them and attempt to flush a few out. If you are ready to get rid of some old industrial worker ideas and replace them with dynamic entrepreneurial ideas, then read on.

THE RISE OF THE GLOBAL SMALL BUSINESS

Almost every business can be a multinational now. Tiny little businesses can behave big. There are millions of 'global small businesses' that have emerged.

A global small business (GSB) isn't like a big global business, and neither is it like a traditional small business. As the name suggests, this is a business with less than 50 staff and it isn't limited by geography. It can reach into cities all over the world and can easily make millions in sales despite a relatively small headcount.

Most commonly, GSBs are service providers, or offer intangible products like software and information. However, many sell high-value physical products that get sent whizzing all over the globe to customers in faraway cities.

A lot of GSBs have valuable intellectual property and media they are known for.

Global small businesses have incredibly well-developed brands compared to traditional small businesses, making them look much bigger than they are. They have a potent culture that holds together a distributed team of people who work remotely from all over the world.

They are built around a focused 'micro-niche'. They don't define themselves by geography, they define themselves by the outcomes they produce, the values they hold dear and the type of people they serve (wherever they might be).

GSBs are exceptional with social media. They interact with the world through online videos, blogs, podcasts, downloads, streaming live events, presentations and communities.

A GSB revolves around the special talents of a few key people of influence. These businesses outsource or automate every function that is not their unique way of creating value.

Inside the team you'll find communications experts, community managers, technology developers and product creators. Everyone shares the passion of the business, the customers and the team.

These GSB teams are not fixed in a geographical location. They communicate on instant messaging apps and social media platforms, manage their operations in the cloud and are technically headquartered wherever it makes sense from a tax and IP protection standpoint.

With a team spread across multiple time zones, the edges of work and play blur for a GSB. Performance is more important than hours. GSBs are the attractive alternative to white-collar corporate employment. Professionals such as lawyers, accountants, consultants and managers are already leaving traditional employment in favour of their own GSB start-up, or to join a GSB that stirs up their underlying passion.

Lifestyle and flexibility are a huge advantage of being part of a GSB. Correctly structured, the owners of GSBs can pay less tax compared to their employee counterparts. Many GSB team members are physically located in low tax, high-lifestyle countries because they can work from anywhere.

Being part of a GSB creates an enviable lifestyle. A GSB isn't like having a traditional, local small business that prevents the owner from travelling and limits the money they can make to the local economy.

A GSB, on the contrary, *expands* as you travel and is only limited by the size of the niche and the creativity of the team. Many GSBs earn millions in revenue and have only a few staff (some of whom are based in low-labour-cost countries such as the Philippines or India). They leverage the latest media and technology to automate and scale the value they deliver. For this reason, many GSBs generate seven-figure profits with comparative ease.

The GSB is an exciting new category of business that has emerged as the barriers to entry drop for doing business across borders.

Being part of the Entrepreneur Revolution begins when you either start or join a GSB.

You won't be tied to a location and you won't have a traditional boss looking over your shoulder. You'll have the power to log into your business from your smartphone anywhere in the world. You will be able to see sales figures, workflow and financials instantly. Your boss will be your customers and the results that appear on your business dashboard.

You will have customers all over the world. Travelling for fun will expand your impact and your bank balance.

Your business won't sleep. You'll be making money 24/7 and you'll have clients in time zones that wrap around the world.

All of this is made possible by the times we are in. The foundations have been laid for people like yourself to unfold your passion into a highly functional business that delivers a ton of value to the world.

IT'S TIME TO CHOOSE

It sounds idealistic. However, it's entirely realistic. These are the times we live in. You have the power and the choice to leave the Industrial Revolution model of employment and become more empowered and free.

The two systems co-exist side by side for now, so it is your choice which one you want to operate in. You can struggle to keep a traditional job and live with the fear of being 'downsized' or having a wage that doesn't keep up with inflation if you really want to.

I attend dinner parties with both groups of people. At the table, my friends working in well-known corporations in traditional roles complain about a lack of job security and inadequate retirement plans. They aren't fulfilled in their work, they find it hard to move up the ladder and they aren't able to save enough money for holidays, a home or the retirement they want. They have to play along with the latest nonsense initiative they secretly believe is a waste of resource. Despite their standout performance, they miss out on promotions because they don't tick the latest made up criteria from up above. They feel like their organisations have become creepy and restrictive places where looking good is more important than going somewhere.

Around the same table are also my entrepreneurial friends. They talk about their latest product launch, their new technology and the freedom it's brought them. They are in control of their destiny and feel fulfilled in life. Also, they have discovered that they can make exponentially more money in their own business than in a job, and they don't feel the need to retire but if they sold their company they could. They care about results and performance in their team and the quality of the ideas that people share.

The Industrial Revolution employment model is a dying animal. It's fundamentally not right for the times we live in. The entrepreneurial GSB is nimble, dynamic and rewarding.

The choice is in your hands because now we are at a turning point in history. Technology has been building and building like a giant wave. This wave has grown in size and speed and we are seeing the convergence of several unrelated ideas bump into each other and create massive, unpredictable results.

Breakthrough technologies are all bumping into each other, resulting in remarkable disruption to the status quo. Smartphones, cloud computing, voice recognition, social media influence, collaborative workspace, virtual reality, resource capacity sharing, video conferencing, large language models, crowdfunding, automation, robots, DNA sequencing, 3D printing, blockchain, facial and gesture recognition, machine learning . . . and the list goes on and on.

Each of these ideas, on its own, has the power to shift industries; but it's bigger than that. These technologies are all integrating with each other to reshape our world.

A great wave of change is dividing two types of people.

1. Those who are surfing this wave into the Entrepreneur Revolution.
2. Those who are clinging to the rocks of the Industrial Revolution and who are in serious trouble whether they know it or not.

As dramatic as it sounds, I believe there's just a brief window of time for people to 'get with the programme' or risk getting left behind.

Artificial intelligence, in particular, has the ability to really drive a wedge. It has two superpowers – the power to get people to consume more than they intended to and the power to get people to create more than they ever could. Some people use AI to generate content and media that propels their businesses forward at speed while others are being secretly manipulated by AI to waste time scrolling social media or buying things they don't need.

As AI becomes more widely deployed, it will become too hard for many people to make the shift from consumer to creator. The people who joined the entrepreneur revolution early will already be adept at leveraging this technology to move forward at light speed by comparison. Time is running out for traditional businesses and jobs that aren't adapting – you must make a deliberate choice to step out of your comfort zone today.

If you're reading this book, I dare say you're committed to stepping away from the old paradigms and towards the new.

If so, let's begin to take some steps forward into the Entrepreneur Revolution. If you're ready, turn the page and let's begin the journey.

Case Study: Changing Mindset

Tom is a fitness trainer who charges an hourly rate and he has a passion for football. His clients typically want to train before and after work so Tom's workday often starts at 6am and goes through to 8pm with a quiet time in the middle of the day. Working this way leaves little time for much else and Tom's relationships suffer and months go by without playing the game he loves.

At first, Tom thought the fitness business would be fun but he's losing his passion and becoming resentful. For Tom, more money means more hard work. He's also scared to charge more because he knows money is tight for everyone right now. He wants to be fair with his clients and doesn't want to be seen as greedy.

Tom's mindset shifts from being a fitness trainer to being an entrepreneur. He starts to realise that people don't want his time, they want better fitness. People love his energy and passion for fitness and they like the accountability and added fun of a trainer. Tom begins to notice that his clients typically have more energy, gain more respect and earn more money when they are fit. Some of his clients have better relationships with their spouses and kids as a result of fitness. He sees that his service is providing great value to people – a lot more than he charges.

As a result of this mindset shift, Tom makes a few key entrepreneurial decisions. He selects high-end clients who are happy to pay more and train during the day. His energy is high again and his clients feel energised by him. His top clients can easily pay a higher rate and Tom doesn't need to do longer hours.

Tom uses some of his free time to create resources that people can access online and he starts building a niche business helping football players to improve their on-field endurance. He attracts a few collaborators to this project and the little team of four people start building an online 'Football Fitness' community who pay for courses and a membership.

A year after his mindset shifted, he found himself with half the fitness training clients willing to pay twice as much and a thriving online business serving a global community of people who share a passion for football. All of these positive changes started when Tom's mindset shifted. Rather than seeing money as hard work, he saw it as an exchange of value – and as soon as he started having more fun he spotted opportunities that were perfect for him.

CHAPTER 2

AWAKEN YOUR ENTREPRENEUR MIND

Your brain controls the way you think and the way you think controls what you do.

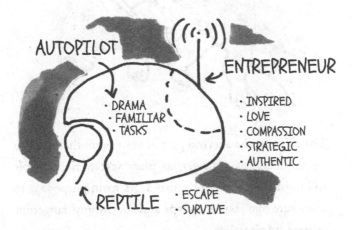

What you do largely gives you the results you see in the outside world; including your bank balance, your house, your car, the types of holidays you go on and the difference you make.

So, if you want to consistently make things happen, it's vitally important that we take a look at the brain and how it's wired.

The brain is incredibly complex, and an exciting piece of kit to learn about properly. If you happen to be a brain-scientist forgive me for oversimplifying things but what I am about to discuss is designed to be useful for entrepreneurs rather than accurate to brain-scientists.

There are three key parts of your 'entrepreneur brain':

1. **The Reptile:** the survival part of your brain that has you see the world as a dangerous place where most people and most things can't be trusted. Its main purpose is to make sure that you can escape and survive any dangerous or stressful situation.
2. **The Autopilot:** the functional worker part of your brain that has you see the world as a set of challenges and problems for you to overcome in exchange for rewards.

3. **The Entrepreneur**: the entrepreneur part of your brain
   has you see a world full of meaningful problems that can
   be solved to create value for others.

DON'T LET THE REPTILE RUN YOUR LIFE

If you operate from the primitive, survival part of your brain,
you can expect to live like a reptile. Reptiles fight for survival, they're always ready to scurry away in fright or get into
a vicious fight over something small. It's not the way to live.

Operating from the survival brain gives you more scarcity in the times we are living in. This part of the brain has no
empathy for others, a skill that is vital in value creation. The
reptile isn't able to reason effectively and it has no concept
of long-term thinking. It's not a logical or strategic part of
the brain; it is programmed to seek out situations that seem
good for immediate survival with as little effort as possible.

The reptile is emotional. It throws tantrums and
wants revenge one minute. The next minute it wants
food or sex. It lashes out at people who are trying to help.
It does reckless things for short-term gains. It sees the
worst in every situation and finds ways to derail progress
without thinking.

The reptile is easily fooled in these modern times with
vices like gambling, pornography, junk food and get-rich-
quick scams. It's the part of the brain that will gamble on
slot machines for hours on end, trading small coins for the
hope of many coins, but it will never compute the folly of
this activity.

The reptile believes the only resources that exist are those it can touch right now. If it can't see money, there's no money. If it can't see food, there's no food.

The reptile will destroy everything around itself if it thinks it will bring an immediate benefit to its survival. If you have ever lashed out at someone close to you, if you have ever smashed something valuable or sent a venomous email that later cost you dearly, it was you 'having a reptile moment'.

THE AUTOPILOT WON'T TAKE YOU TO NICE DESTINATIONS

The autopilot brain isn't much better than the reptile brain if you want to achieve success as an entrepreneur.

If you operate from the purely functional part of your brain, you will live life on repeat. You will have friends and you will be able to perform repetitive tasks, but most of what you do will not be very meaningful in the long term.

You will do what you need to do to get through the week. You'll watch Netflix, order takeout, turn up to meetings, pay your bills, drop the kids at school and make pleasant conversation with a friend. It will all turn into a blur though – devoid of passion and meaning, you put one foot after the next foot without thinking much about where you're going.

The autopilot part yearns for 'passive income'. It wants a simple system that brings in money on autopilot. Anything that looks repeatable and easy appeals to this part of the brain. It loves the idea that one day, money will just arrive automatically and permanently so that it can finally relax. The autopilot believes the only resources it can access are those it's been told it can access. If you tell the autopilot it earns $85,000 a year, it believes that's all there is. If you tell the autopilot it has a credit card limit of $4500, that's it until a letter arrives from the bank saying that it's now $5000.

If you've ever found months pass by and you have nothing much to show for it, you've been 'on autopilot'. If you have goals, dreams, hopes and wishes that go unfulfilled year after year you're probably stuck in this mode.

THE VISIONARY ENTREPRENEUR BUILDS AN EMPIRE

If you want to build something of real value that expands, you need to access your entrepreneur brain.

If you operate from the entrepreneurial part of your brain you will build a little empire. You will develop a space that is truly your own, people will be honoured to share conversations with you, you will solve big important problems and make a difference to many people.

The entrepreneur part of your brain has great amounts of empathy, logic, reasoning and higher consciousness. These are all great skills for building your empire.

Your expansive entrepreneur brain has a capacity to love the world. It can connect with people and events over vast distances. It can calculate future events, it can draw unique insights from your own past or even the stories of others and naturally devise strategies. It's wise beyond the comprehension of the autopilot or the reptile.

While reptiles believe in resources they can touch and autopilots believe what they are told, the entrepreneur believes that if a resource exists on the planet, it's possible to influence how that resource is used.

An entrepreneur believes that their empire grows when they have greater influence over resources but they care not who technically 'owns' the resource. They use other people's money, fame, credibility and time to get things done.

If you have ever had moments of pure inspiration where you feel anything is possible, you want to start a movement and do something meaningful for humanity, you were having a 'visionary entrepreneur' moment.

Do Not Stimulate Your Reptile Brain!

If you want to destroy everything you have, stimulate your reptile mind regularly. Engaging in negative self-talk whereby you tell yourself, over and again, how scarce things are and how tough life is will do it. Telling yourself that you are barely surviving and there are no resources around you gets the reptile riled up rapidly.

If you really want to stimulate the reptile, keep an empty fridge, have no access to cash so your reptile is always on edge. Check your phone all the time and look at the worst things happening in society. Log into porn sites or use social media to follow people who make you feel angry, unhappy and small. Then deny yourself rewards for your efforts so your reptile feels like nothing is working.

All of these things stimulate the reptile brain, which will push you to the brink of reptile behaviour. You will act aggressively to those who are closest to you, you will take stupid, short-term actions that come back to bite you and you will spiral out of control.

In order to try to stop the spiral you will construct an unattainable fantasy. In your fantasy, you might imagine yourself with passive income, retirement and big winnings.

In these fantasies, you probably don't have to do anything and money keeps rolling in. This fantasy is designed as a safety mechanism to try to stop you completely destroying yourself.

Unfortunately, the fantasy is a juvenile approach to life and it causes you to spend what little money or time you have on quick-fix solutions that won't work. You might join a multi-level marketing operation that you won't give any time to, you put money into a high-risk investment you don't understand, you gamble or you spend money trying to look rich to create the fantasy.

It's easy to spot these reptile fantasies. They are typically presented to you as:

Passive income. The reptile imagines that money comes from a source that requires no time, energy, effort or focus. The entrepreneur knows that making money and building a successful business will always require energy, time and effort. However, if you are dedicated to a meaningful cause it will be fulfilling, rewarding and ethical.

Retirement. The reptile wants you to squirrel away money that you believe you will live on after you are too old 'to hunt or gather'. The entrepreneur never wants to retire, but looks to making a contribution for as many years as possible.

Multiple streams of income. The reptile enjoys fantasising about money coming from many sources, thus 'safeguarding your food supply'. The entrepreneur loves to focus on earning money from sources that fit perfectly with your mission and your vision; if it's one source or twenty, the entrepreneur cares not.

Big wins. The reptile likes the idea of making all the money you need for the rest of your life in one hit. The entrepreneur doesn't try to get everything done in one hit, because they realise that consistently creating regular wins creates the big jumps.

Entitlements. Your reptile brain believes there's money that 'should rightfully be yours'. The entrepreneur believes that money is energy and will flow towards people who earn the right to utilise it best.

Providers. The reptile wants a person or organisation who will take care of you and then you won't need to worry about money. The entrepreneur is looking for organisations, causes and people to provide for.

Financial freedom. The reptile imagines a time when you will not need to be responsible for money and thus be free from it. The entrepreneur recognises and embraces the need to tackle the financial complexity that's created along with wealth.

Of course, all of these are juvenile concepts created by clever people who know how to sell ideas to reptiles and monkeys.

The only people who have these things are entrepreneurial empire builders. However, they don't even relate to these concepts. They just think about building an empire.

For starters, entrepreneurs never retire. They do all they can to work as long as they can – often they stop 'working' just weeks before they die.

They don't see themselves as beneficiaries of passive income or multiple streams of income. They see they are in service of one growing empire that has much to be cared for.

They don't go for easy, quick wins. They take on the big challenges and, when they do have a big win, they find another big challenge to take on next.

They don't seek out financial freedom, they manage financial complexity. They don't look for a provider, they look for opportunities to provide for others.

Getting Back in Control

Here's the problem. The brain was built in such a way that the lower parts of the mind can shut down the higher parts. If the reptile brain is overstimulated it shorts out the auto-pilot and entrepreneur, and it takes over.

In a survival situation, you don't want to empathise with your attacker, nor do you want to continue going through the motions. You want to do what's needed to survive and nothing else. So the reptile is in charge when you feel your survival is threatened.

If the reptile part of the brain returns to calm again, the repetitive autopilot takes over and gets on with its daily existence that revolves around repetitive tasks. The autopilot brain is in charge when you do not feel like your survival is immediately threatened and there's an endless to-do list to work on.

Provided there's plenty of tasks, the autopilot brain stays stimulated, you cannot access the higher mind of the visionary entrepreneur. Your inner empire builder only comes out when you truly feel abundant, centred and inspired in the moment.

This realisation may start to give you insights into why society is set up the way that it is.

The people who ran the show in the Industrial Revolution did not want very many entrepreneurs running around. Many parts of society during the Industrial Revolution evolved to keep people from going into 'survival mode' and tearing the streets up like savage reptiles. Governments set up provision for social security, pensions and healthcare because, without these ideas, the population might feel their very survival was under threat and end up burning down the city just trying to survive winter.

After survival is taken care of, the system is designed to keep people performing like well-trained little machines, who can perform mind-numbing, repetitive tasks for years on end. Good factory workers.

Most importantly, the system seems to have been set up to keep people from spending time in their higher mind – the empire building part.

Entrepreneurs pose a threat to powerful industrialists; if an entrepreneur is in business they can take your market share (like Richard Branson, Steve Jobs or Oprah Winfrey did); or, if they are a humanitarian, they can liberate your workers (like Gandhi, Bobby Kennedy, Martin Luther King Jr).

In order to keep workers as workers, and to prevent them from rising up, two things must happen:

1. People must be convinced that they are able to survive. You must not threaten their survival in the immediate moment or they will turn savage and behave like reptiles; but you must ensure that people feel that they aren't abundant just yet.

2. People must be kept occupied with tasks or entertainment so that they don't have a chance to access their higher mind. Not only will this prevent people from becoming disruptive, but also the stimulated reptile brain loves to consume shiny new objects that it gets bored with rapidly. The stimulated reptile brain creates wonderful consumers in the economy.

Does this sound familiar? It should: it's exactly how the masses have been treated for the last 200 years. The mainstream news, entertainment and popular personalities all reinforce these two messages.

The traditional, mainstream media is an elegant way to keep most people out of their visionary entrepreneur brain.

For good measure they even mock the idea of ordinary people being entrepreneurial in popular media all the time.

If you look at the way we are bombarded by advertising and entertainment, it's no wonder so few people ever escape their emotions or meaningless tasks.

When you look at what's really going on in society, we have built global systems to keep people on the treadmill.

If we examine almost every spiritual teaching that gives you a path to enlightenment, the advice is fairly simple – tune out from all the stimulation for a while and give yourself a chance to access your higher mind.

Spiritual teachers often suggest going to a very safe place and fasting, meditating, being silent and celibate for a while. It's all about avoiding the stimulation of tasks and distractions.

When people tune out from the noise, they give themselves a chance to access their inner entrepreneur. They tap into new ideas that could help people, and they discover vast resources they barely knew existed.

Accessing your visionary entrepreneur mind isn't as hard as you might think. You need to do two things:

1. Avoid the things that make you emotional and stop doing meaningless tasks.
2. Be grateful for where you are in this moment.

When you awaken your entrepreneur brain you'll start seeing just how much opportunity is surrounding you right now. You'll see how society is built to keep you focused on playing small rather than reaching your full potential.

ACTIVITY: WHO IS BEING SELFISH?

Let's play a game.

Pick a number. This number is an amount of money you want to earn in the next 12 months. It should be a number that satisfies your wants and needs for the next year but isn't greedy.

Imagine that any number you write, as if by magic, will be your income – to do with as you wish without further conditions. You can write any amount you want as long as you aren't greedy or selfish.

Choose the amount you want and write it down:

$ _____

NOTE: Do it now, don't read on until you've got a number in mind.

How much did you choose? Was it twice your salary, three times or did you go wild and write down something like a telephone number?

The instructions were clear. You had to choose a number that isn't 'greedy or selfish'.

If you wrote down a number less than a billion dollars I'm disappointed and we have a lot of work to do on your 'empire-building' mindset. Less than a billion indicates that you are too greedy and selfish to be fully functional in the Entrepreneur Revolution.

Too 'Greedy' and 'Selfish'!?

Why would I accuse you of that (if you wrote down less than a billion)? After all, if you are like most people your number was probably modest, you didn't ask for vast sums, you were reasonable.

Well, here is the thing. I said 'an amount that would satisfy all your wants and needs'.

If you only thought about your own personal desires, your amount would be a small amount. It would be greedy and selfish by definition to only think about your own circumstances. If you thought about your family, the amount would be bigger but still fairly small. If you thought about the big issues we face as a planet your amount would have been trillions!

Choosing a bigger amount would allow you to impact more people.

I am really hoping you have wants and needs that extend past you and your family. I hope you want to save rainforests, end hunger in faraway countries, influence policy, set up foundations, empower economically poor people, rescue animals or something much bigger than yourself.

You just can't do that with an amount like $10 million.

With $10 million you could have a nice home, a nice car, a nice holiday, make a nice little donation and invest a nice little amount for your future and pay some nice taxes.

That is it. You're barely able to do nice things for your extended family, your community, your local elderly, your local environment.

My answer is a little different.

I answer that question like this:

I want the most amount of money that I can receive as a result of me adding value to others and being true to my purpose and passions.

If I am lucky enough to be like Elon Musk and my passion makes me a billionaire then I will rise to the challenges that billions calls for.

If my passion makes only a small amount of money but I am self-governing, free and I am an inspiration to myself and others then I will accept that too.

The important point is that it's not selfish to have a lot of spare time or a lot of spare cash. It's selfish to indulge all of your time doing something that neither serves or inspires anyone and then make a boring amount of money that only barely compensates you for your time.

THE POOR MINDSET IS THE GREEDY MINDSET

Why do most people choose a small amount of money? It's because they believe money requires hard work and more income must require more hard work. It's also because they believe money is scarce and limited and having money must in some way detract from the experience of others.

Elite families don't feel this way. They are raised to believe that money arises when value is delivered. Money is a unit for measuring a transfer of value and that value is not linked to their hard work. Value could be delivered through systems, products, access to property or unique connections.

Elite families also teach their kids an important secret – money is made up. It's a human invention akin to a database and the database is edited by humans all the time who simply make up more money. Every time you take a loan from a bank, the bankers just make up the loan in the database. Every time a government has a massive objective it's committed to, it goes and makes up the money for that thing – we witnessed this during the 2008 global financial crisis and the Covid-19 pandemic.

People who were raised in elite families don't link money to work and they know money is not a zero sum game. To them, money isn't real in the same way it is for most people.

If you ask a rich person, 'What would you do for £10,000?' they would say, 'It's not about the money – I do things that are important to me.'

If you ask a poor person, 'What will you do for $1000?' they quickly demonstrate how easily they are bought. For $10,000 most people will give up the best part of their week for a vision that doesn't inspire them, working with people they barely care about and perform a role that is repetitive and dull. Most people will stay in a job they hate if the money is good enough.

Controversially, it is the poor-minded person who is acting greedy and selfish around money.

It is the people with a rich mindset who are mostly indifferent to the stuff. They are only interested in their vision, their passion, their companions, their adventure.

In the Entrepreneur Revolution, you must be true to your convictions. If you're easily bought, you'll end up stuck in a dead-end job and a race to the bottom.

ACTIVITY: WHAT DO YOU DO FOR A LIVING?

What do you currently do for a living? Write it down:

_____

NOTE: *Don't read on until you have written down your answer.*

What did you write? Did you put down sales executive, area manager, plumber, tree surgeon, town planner, consultant or architect?

Did you write down your job? Your occupation? Your source of income?

Why? Why did you write that? Why do most people think that what they do for income is what keeps them alive?

It's not! What keeps you alive is not your job title.

If you ask an American Inuit tribesman what he does for a living he will look at you strangely and say, 'I breathe.'

At least in the short term. After that I guess he will need some water, some good food, a good night's rest and an active day filled with a sense of adventure to keep him living.

After 200 years of conditioning we now answer with our job title.

The factory owners of the Industrial Revolution wanted their staff to be clear of one thing: 'working in my factory keeps you alive, working here is linked to living'. They wanted us to fear leaving the factory so they could pay people just enough to survive.

In the Entrepreneur Revolution we kiss goodbye to this irrational survival fear of 'not having enough to live'. We have built up a fear that what we do for income is keeping us alive; but now we must move beyond it. It isn't logical and it doesn't serve us anymore.

It is an idea that the wealthy families don't have. If you asked Prince William what he did for a living he would be confused. When you explained that you were asking about how he sustained his place in the economy, he would tell you that he is royalty and has an empire and he reigns over it. It's unlikely he thinks he 'works at the palace for a living'.

Even self-made people are different. They hate being asked that question. As an entrepreneur who's passionate about their business it doesn't feel like you're doing things to 'make a living' and survive. The truth is you do a lot of stuff and it all seems to be in service of a vision you have. The truth is wealthy people kind of 'reign' over their little empires more than they 'work for a crust'.

If you asked me what I physically do for income my answer isn't so simple. I now have multiple business interests, I am an international public speaker, I'm an author, I have investments. It is my little empire.

More to the point, it's not what I do for an income. I do this stuff because it's in line with my vision, it's part of my adventure and I am inspired to do it. It creates value so it produces income as well.

I don't have to show up for work; I want to play this game.

We need to start thinking differently. We must stop thinking like workers and start thinking like entrepreneurs.

When you think about what you do for a living you start to think about your passion, your purpose and your vision. Don't think about your job, your income and your pension plan.

When you think bigger you will cease to be an unimportant worker who's surviving, you'll become an entrepreneur who is building an empire.

A STATE OF MONEY OR A STATE OF MIND?

Of course, it is all just a state of mind – one that affects your most important decisions. Changing your mindset about money and business is a choice you can make at any time. With new information about the times we are in you can instantly update your mindset to recognise that you are here to have an adventure, to play a fun game and to create value.

Entrepreneurship begins with a mindset shift. You are changing from someone who believes hard work creates money to someone who sees money as nothing more than a placeholder for value. Creating more value for more people will expand the amount of money that flows around you. A business is a vehicle for creating and distributing value and managing the flow of money related to that value. An entrepreneur creates and expands that vehicle so it delivers more value to more people.

An entrepreneur doesn't do hard work, they breathe life-force energy into a business venture. They spark the creation of value and the flow of money. In doing so, they create an entity that takes on a life of its own – a business.

To awaken this part of your mind, it's not enough to simply think differently. You must start to do things differently. In the next chapter we will explore 10 actions that transform you into a more entrepreneurial person.

Do you have an entrepreneurial mindset? Answer the quiz and find out. You will get customised feedback and suggestions about how to enhance your entrepreneurial outlook.

www.dent.global/er-quiz

Do You have What it Takes?

Most people will go through their entire life working in a job feeling powerless to take charge of their own destiny. If you're going to be different, you'd better be ready for the challenges that come before the glory. Don't even embark on the journey of entrepreneurship unless you have the following three ingredients.

1. Willingness to Stretch

The very fact that you wish to create something new (a new lifestyle, a new product, a new business, a new result) means that you need to accept that it doesn't currently exist within your sphere of influence. If it did, you wouldn't be creating it. If you're creating something new, don't be shocked when it requires you to stretch.

Creating something worthwhile means that it will require more money than is in your current bank account, it will require more time than you have spare and it will require you to perform at a level you don't currently know how to. This means you're going to have to get used to being stretched.

You need to embrace the feeling of being stretched. Every time you feel that you're being pulled into the unknown, or there's too much to do, you need to smile and remember that this is what it feels like to be doing something big and meaningful.

Remember that you're the one who chose this journey and you knew it was going to require you to stretch. If you're stretched then it means things are working out the way you planned!

Entrepreneurship isn't a ticket to riches. It is a bumpy road that can end up smooth if things go well. A lot of people online gloat about their easy life as an entrepreneur; you can be guaranteed this came at a cost. Every successful entrepreneur is stretched to their limits at times – especially at the beginning. Start the journey only if you accept this is going to take you out of your comfort zone.

2. WILLINGNESS TO GET RESOURCEFUL

The way you deal with being stretched is to get resourceful. Rather than dwelling in the discomfort of how you are being stretched, you get proactive about finding a solution.

Being stretched triggers your reptile brain but only your visionary brain can see solutions. Entrepreneurs are often in a mental battle to quiet their reptile brain so their entrepreneurial instincts can kick in and get a breakthrough.

Very few people care about your complaints; they are too busy doing their own thing. Most successful people believe that if you live in a developed economy you don't have much to complain about, you just need to get on with it.

If you lose your temper and act out as an entitled, temperamental brat you will set yourself back by months or years depending on who sees it. Self-awareness, self-control and time to regain your composure are an important part of being an entrepreneur who can stay resourceful.

By definition, entrepreneurs never have the resources they need to succeed. They are always looking for ways to unlock them. They have to keep their minds calm and their eyes open to possibilities.

Once you're in a resourceful state and you are having resourceful conversations, it's just a matter of sticking to the path. After you know what needs doing, you must be willing to be held accountable for getting the results.

3. Willingness to be Held Accountable

You will produce better results when you are held account-able. When you have deadlines to meet, you will do what needs to be done to hit them. When you have someone you respect pushing you to create your best work, you create your best work.

Most people know how to exercise and how to eat healthier meals. The reason we don't do it is because we don't have anyone else holding us to account.

When people get a fitness trainer they suddenly start eating better and exercising every week because they have someone checking in on them, not because they have sud-denly learned what to eat and how to exercise.

This principle applies to anything you want to do that requires you to stretch and to be resourceful. Your autopilot brain wants to do things that are familiar. It isn't a great ally when it comes to stretching and getting resourceful. Your autopilot brain is happier checking Facebook, answering emails or chatting with friends.

A big motivator for many people to become an entrepre-neur is the perceived freedom they will gain. This freedom can come once your business has built effective systems, developed valuable assets and attracted a competent team. Until then, it's up to you to keep doing the right things knowing that there is a massive delay in the gratification you'll experience.

You need an external motivational force to keep you on track. Your entrepreneur brain needs an ally so it can over-throw the autopilot and the reptile.

This ally comes in the form of external accountability. You need someone else to reorientate you back to the original intention of creating something big, exciting and meaningful. Without this support structure it's too easy to just play small or go back to what you know.

As you stretch, and as you get resourceful, you need external accountability to sustain you long enough to get results.

If you are OK with these three things, we can proceed to take steps to really awaken your entrepreneurial mindset and start a business that works.

CHAPTER 3

TEN CHALLENGES TO SPARK YOUR ENTREPRENEURIAL TALENTS

You now have a problem. If you are reading a book like this, you've already woken up the entrepreneurial part of you and it makes you restless.

You yearn to do big, meaningful work. You want to cause an impact. You want progress and transformation.

This will not go away; the restlessness will heighten if you don't act upon it. If you trust my process, you won't just wake up your inner entrepreneur – you will live that way.

Rather than just talking about the mindset let's begin some real-life challenges to activate your entrepreneur mind.

I'm going to introduce you to ten tasks that are designed to challenge you. These tasks aren't theory. As you'll see, I've done each of them myself.

I've recommended these ten tasks to numerous friends and consistently the feedback is that they are transformational.

These ten tasks aren't just fun things to read about, they must be completed. You will need to 'do' these things to get the lessons.

Even if you think you can imagine what it would be like to complete these tasks – do them for real.

I promise you that, if you do, you will rapidly begin to flush out the industrialised worker mentality and open yourself up to a world of new opportunities. Magic will happen.

CHALLENGE 1: MAKE THREE CALLS

Begin something bold without knowing how, exactly, it will work out. You might want to plan an event, you might want to launch a cafe or perhaps build software you think might solve a problem. Whatever it is, don't plan ahead, begin it and let it unfold AFTER you're moving in the direction. Make three phone calls and see what happens.

Let me take you back to the beginning of my entrepreneurial journey and walk you through some critical lessons.

In the first year of university, I came up with an idea to run a dance party for 15–17 year olds. The more I researched it and created clever and cheap ways to market the party, the more it seemed like an entirely valid idea.

I was excited but didn't know what to do next. I called up my dad, explained the situation and asked him what I should do; and he said 'make three calls'.

His suggestion was simple: make three phone calls to see if anyone else is interested in your idea. Not friends, not family, but three people who will either advance the idea forward or tell you why it's not for them.

My first call was to a warehouse rental company that had a big green shed across the street in my local park. They told me that it wasn't a suitable venue and that they tried to have an 18th birthday party there once and it was a disaster. They suggested I call an actual nightclub venue.

My second call was more ambitious. I called the top nightclub in town.

To my surprise, the receptionist put me through to the general manager. In my most professional voice I introduced myself and said 'I am from a dance party promotions company and we have selected your nightclub as a possible venue for our launch party for under-18s. You're normally closed on a Tuesday night, I'm thinking about running something in the first week of school holidays with you.'

He didn't hang up on me, nor did he get excited. He simply asked me to send through a proposal and then organise a time to meet with him through his assistant.

'I can't send you a proposal today because I am out of the office, but I will have one to you tomorrow.'

My third call was back to my dad to find out what a proposal was.

My friends and I met with the nightclub manager and he agreed to run the party. As we walked out the door, he asked if we had thought about radio ads.

We didn't have any money for radio ads but we used my dad's advice again and made three calls to local radio stations.

A few meetings later, I'd secured $4000 of free advertising in exchange for the naming rights of the party. The radio station suggested we should get some prizes from retail stores. I made three more calls and found retailers who were happy to give us over $1000 worth of prizes.

The retail stores suggested we have a fashion parade. I made three calls and found that one of the girls in my class was a model who knew how to run a fashion parade. She suggested we go out for drinks together and I made three calls to brag to my friends!

The party was a huge success and my friend and I both walked away with more cash than we could carry that night.

This became our sideline business and we were both able to make good spending money while at university.

On that first day, I never knew how it would unfold, I just made those calls to see what would happen next. I hadn't a clue what we would be getting ourselves into but it felt great to begin it. With each step forward the next steps appeared and before long we had an exciting result.

I'm not saying you should be reckless, I'm saying that it's impossible to know how things will pan out until after you begin. Take the first steps, pick up the phone and put yourself out there.

Your inner entrepreneur is OK with sitting in the tension of uncertainty. The entrepreneur knows that resources show up when they are needed and normally not beforehand. The entrepreneur understands that clarity comes at the end of the show not the beginning.

Entrepreneurs believe that they have access to any resources that exist on the planet, whenever they need it, and that they only need to have the right conversations about how they are used.

To action this task, think of a business idea you'd like to explore, send some emails or direct messages to people who could help make it happen and arrange some quick calls. The message doesn't have to be complicated – 'I'm at the early stages of launching a product and I think it's something we could discuss working with you, can we have a 15 minute call to discuss it?' Begin the conversation without knowing where it will lead you.

The entrepreneur needs to be OK with stepping into the unknown and having an adventure. To the entrepreneur the whole world is a stage and everyone is a fellow player in the game of life.

The entrepreneur isn't scared, but the autopilot and the reptile get terrified if there's no predictability. If they feel threatened, the reptile and the autopilot will do everything they can to hold the entrepreneur back.

Challenge 2: Get Your Reptile Brain a Bank Account

Set up a new bank account and put 10% of all the money you earn into that account. This 'reptile account' helps you to feel OK about taking risks, and will eventually stop you from needing to go do boring, familiar tasks. Don't touch that money; its purpose is nothing more than to become part of 'your wealth'. This wealth-building plan will be an essential key for keeping the reptile off your back.

After the success of our first dance party, my best mate and I were thoroughly convinced we were going to be successful entrepreneurs. We talked endlessly about how, one day, we would have expensive cars, big boats and houses all over the world. We were planning out our dreams and it was exciting.

His dad saw we had made some money and took us aside and gave us some interesting advice. He said 'be sure to put 10% aside and then you can go blow the rest on whatever you want'.

It was shocking advice coming from an adult. Weren't we meant to invest it all, or pay off some debt (not that we had any) or save it up for a distant rainy day?

He was a clever businessman, and he knew it was important to enjoy our earnings while also provisioning 10% into a separate, wealth-building account. He said, 'if you just keep 10% of everything you earn, you'll build your bank balance. Having money puts you in a position to make better choices with your life.'

The reptile brain is risk adverse. It just wants to survive and views everything as a threat.

People will tell you how risky it is to go and do big things like start a business. Having a stash of money, that just keeps growing, helps you to reason with your reptile brain.

You also want your emotional reptile brain to feel safe this money will not be used for any 'big dreams or schemes'. The money you put aside can never be used for business, spending or risky investments. It's for boring stuff like cash, property, shares and metals. It's a mental safety net.

The reptile needs to know your survival is being taken care of, so this account will appease the part of you that's hyper-conservative and safety concerned.

I set up a special account with my bank called 'the reptile account' and 10% of my earnings automatically go into it.

When my account got to a certain size (about 3 months of living costs) I started moving the extra money into a basic share portfolio fund – nothing sexy, nothing risky.

It just keeps ticking along, every month money goes in and does its boring job of keeping my brain quiet. As an added bonus, these boring investments have done well. My shares seem to double and double every decade, staying well ahead of inflation.

I hardly look at it and it always shocks me to see how much it adds up to over time. It makes me feel very calm to know that I have cash to fall back on if I need it, as well as boring investments in the wider economy.

I've noticed when I put money aside I don't actually miss it. I have lived on yachts, had penthouse apartments, travelled the world, eaten in the best restaurants and driven prestige cars. I've never once thought 'I'm 10% short for what I want to do'.

After getting married and having kids I took additional precautions to keep our family safe while taking entrepreneurial risks. I have insurances, emergency credit cards and written instructions in the event of a worst case scenario. These things are designed to keep my reptile brain calm so I can get on with being the best entrepreneur I can be.

You'll see that if you can keep your reptile calm, your entrepreneur plans will be better planned and executed. You'll easily see ways to move up in the world and spend time with other people who have a big entrepreneur mindset.

CHALLENGE 3: STOP SPENDING TIME WITH PEOPLE WHO BRING YOU DOWN

Start making friends with people who inspire you. Spend time having conversations with people who bring out the best in you. Make a list of people you currently spend a lot of time with and decide who can stay and who needs to go.

You become like the people you have conversations with. These people determine the dominant ideas you ponder, the opportunities you notice and the resources you can access.

If you do not have any people on your list who inspire you, you're better off spending time out networking in inspirational places trying to find some.

Today I'm fortunate to spend a lot of my time with inspiring people. I talk regularly with people who run exciting, fast-growth enterprises, people who lead charities and people who've achieved remarkable things and are addressing meaningful challenges.

Most of my insights come from an ongoing conversation with a peer group of entrepreneurs and change makers.

One of the reasons I dropped out of university was because I realised most people I spent time with were playing small. At the end of my first year in university I became aware that most people I met were struggling to survive. I remember talking to a business lecturer who shared the fact that he and his wife were struggling to pay rent. This scared me. Why am I learning from a guy who's struggling to pay rent?

I could see this was only going to normalise playing small.

I decided to set out and find inspiring mentors to shadow. I figured if I could spend time with wealthy, dynamic, inspiring people, I might actually figure out what they do differently.

It was a frightening move to leave my uni friends and peers. I was afraid I would be alone and wouldn't fit in with another crowd. My parents were both the first in their families to have a university degree and now I was going to become a 'dropout'.

When I was 19 years old I went to work for a friend of a friend named Jon, a successful businessman and marketeer.

Jon's company promoted and ran events all over Australia. He had a big house, a vibrant family and he was engaged in meaningful work. He wore board shorts and sandals most of the time, woke up when his kids did, played lots of games and was great fun to be around.

When he asked me to join his team of 'inspired sales legends', I laughed, because it was a very different way of explaining a job compared to the door-to-door roof insulation company sales team I had been working with on weekends. They simply called me a 'door-knocker'.

The other people who worked for Jon were all interested in achieving big, exciting and meaningful things too. They all read professional and personal development books, had written goals and discussed ways to achieve big goals. The inspired conversations began and my mind tuned into all sorts of new opportunities.

Your environment has a profound impact on you. Making some changes to your peer group can be difficult but once it's done you'll see your life changing as if by magic.

I went from having regular conversations about grocery bills, rent and university deadlines to goals, dreams, plans and sales targets.

After a few weeks I knew that I wanted to learn more so I asked Jon if he could teach me about marketing and business. He agreed and the lessons began.

He taught me about sales, marketing, conducting meetings, doing deals and building wealth. He also taught me how to treat money differently.

CHALLENGE 4: CARRY CASH

Carry $1000 on you at all times. If $1000 isn't enough to make you a little bit uncomfortable, carry the amount you'd love to earn in a day. We need your brain to reorientate what it considers to be pocket money.

One day, my new mentor Jon asked me how much money I considered to be a lot. After some thought I replied, 'There's not much a guy can't do on $1000 a week.'

He laughed, and said that if I was only making $10,000 worth of sales a week (I was on 10%) then he wouldn't keep me on in his company. This excited me no end.

He then instructed me to do something quite strange, which had a powerful impact on my life.

Jon told me to get my hands on $2000 and bring it back to him. I told him that I had $100 in cash, $500 in the bank and I had $1000 limit on my credit card. He said, 'go ask your dad for the rest or something, just bring me $2000 tomorrow'.

I somehow got my hands on this vast sum of money and brought it back to him. Without much of a care he took it off me, stuck a bulldog clip on it and said 'carry that in your pocket at all times'.

It was wild. I was walking down the street feeling like, at any moment, a gang of ninjas would jump me and steal my entire net worth. I was nervous and excited all at once, and my hand never left my pocket for the first few weeks – better safe than sorry.

Then, one day, something strange happened. I was walking past a jewellery store and saw an Omega watch. It was awesome!

CARRY CASH

'It's $2000 . . . you can't afford that', said my autopilot brain. 'Wait a second . . . I have $2000 in my pocket . . . I can afford it right now if I want', my entrepreneur brain responded.

After a brief conversation with myself, I realised that, even though I could afford it, I would choose to wait until I had earned it. I decided that when I had turned over $1 million in my own business I would buy it as a reward. That felt right, and it also made me feel empowered that I had made this decision rather than feeling powerless in view of the watch's price tag.

Over the following 12 months this became a regular occurrence. I would notice something I thought I could not afford and then realised that I actually had enough money in my pocket to buy most things.

All of a sudden, I was in the driver's seat. I had the power over the things and not the other way around. I reduced my emotional charge on money, the idea that $2000 was a lot of money didn't resonate anymore; it's just how much I carried in my pocket.

In the first year working for Jon I went from earning $1200 a month, as a broke university student, to earning $12,000 a month doing something that I considered fun; plus I was living in a gorgeous beach location. Few people take this sort of a jump so quickly, and I believe that the $2000 in the pocket was a big part of that shift.

Carry cash to confront your emotions around money and recalibrate how much your brain thinks is a lot. This activity will do more for you than reading all the money books or attending all the money seminars.

CHALLENGE 5: TAKE SOMEONE NEW OUT TO LUNCH

Take a new person out to lunch each week and pick up the bill. This will build your network and spark opportunities.

My next challenge from Jon was to build a better network of people around me who weren't customers, clients or old friends. To help with this, I had to select one or two new people a week to take out for lunch at my expense. This was tough in the beginning, but wonderful later on.

Initially, I couldn't think of anyone who would want to go to lunch with me, who I would be willing to pay for. I was stalemated by my lack of confidence and my lack of money.

But I had to come up with at least one per week, so I just started asking people who I would never have thought would join me for lunch. Business owners, investors, accountants and authors – I sent them an invite even though I expected most wouldn't even respond.

You'll be surprised how many great people respond favourably when you say 'Can I take you out for lunch next week, it's on me, I don't know you well enough but I'm sure there's plenty of good reason we should be talking.'

To my amazement, most people I invited were quite happy to go out to lunch. I listened to their stories, got great advice, fresh ideas and found myself learning all sorts of new things. I learned to connect with people and discovered what people are going through in life beneath the surface.

I was developing a network and I was able to start introducing people, which made me feel even more valuable.

When I was on a sales call I had all sorts of stories to share and I was speaking from experience and a genuinely inspired place. People would listen to me, and I made more sales.

Often I would get introduced to people as well. I would get referrals, opportunities and advice. Taking people out to lunch wasn't an expense, it was making me money.

When you do this consistently, you will find taking people out to lunch builds a valuable asset – your network. Having a network builds your net worth more than almost anything else.

CHALLENGE 6: TUNE OUT FROM THE NEWS

Unfollow all media and news. No papers, no radio, no TV and no social media feeds. Feel free to Google stories that relate directly to your business, but for at least 90 days avoid news.

On the weekends I would walk down to the local cafe on the beach and order breakfast and a juice and read the newspaper, to catch up on the rest of the world that I had missed out on while I was busily building my little empire through the week.

It was terrible: war, death, accidents, failing businesses, crashing stock markets, rising interest rates, rapists and murderers. This stuff was everywhere!

Well, it wasn't everywhere; a lot of it was happening in other parts of the world. Very few disasters were happening in my little beachside town, no murderers had killed people I knew personally and none of the wars were taking place in my local area.

When I took stock of this fact I realised that none of the news was relevant to my life at all. These events were going to happen with or without my involvement. Even if I was aware of these news stories I wasn't going to do much about it, other than to ride the emotional highs and lows of the story.

I had been led to believe that I needed to be up to date with these world events in order to function in society. I'd been told that news was important and it helped to shape my mind as a free thinker. This isn't as true as it once was – carefully selected books, podcasts and websites are better for your brain.

With encouragement from a mentor, I decided it was safe to tune out from the news. I bought good books for the weekend at the cafe and to completely be carefree from the world events of politics, wars, death and destruction.

And guess what happened? Nothing!

I didn't get surprised by the phantom boogeyman that the papers had been warning me about. I didn't lose all my money in a stock market crash that had been repeatedly foretold on TV. No national draft picked me to fight a war that I hadn't been up to date on. Absolutely nothing happened – except I felt good!

I felt lighter and more empowered. Occasionally, someone would say 'aren't you worried about flying?' and I would say 'No, why would I be?' and they would look at me as if I was either a heroic champion for getting on with things under pressure, or a loony who simply didn't understand the imminent threats associated with the new insurgence of terrorists.

Either way, I made it through the dangerous world just fine.

My reptile brain was terrified of tuning out from the news. It needed the emotional highs and lows and, in the first few weeks, it really kept nagging at me to get a newspaper or switch on the television for an update.

After a while, my reptile brain calmed down and I felt OK about living in a world without a daily download of the statistically improbable events.

News is anything that is interesting but you have no ability to influence. YouTube videos about the economy are just a form of news. Blogs about famous people are just news. Podcasts about politics, even if it relates to business in general, is more news. You don't need it. You need to focus on things you can control.

When you tune out from the news, you will probably feel anxious that you're missing out on something. Quickly you will discover that, if anything does relate to you, someone will tell you about it. After a while, you will be shocked at how much energy you once gave to this thinly veiled form of entertainment.

When I first did this, most of the news was traditional media delivered at intervals throughout the day. Today most people are in constant contact with a newsfeed through their social media and it's nearly impossible to tune out. It requires deleting apps from your phone, unfollowing accounts or even having a friend change your passwords and keep them safely out of your reach.

Instead of getting worried about world events, stay inspired and keep focused on things you can control.

I came to discover my own life was more important than the stories presented to me by some newsroom editor or algorithm.

When I focused on my own life I did things that were newsworthy myself. My life was becoming more interesting and I put value on my own unfolding story.

So much was happening that I decided to start writing it down.

CHALLENGE 7: KEEP AN ENTREPRENEUR JOURNAL

Start an entrepreneur's journal. Make lists of high-value tasks, write down your goals, draw diagrams, write sales copy and project your future. Keep track of your thoughts and mark down your milestones. Every entrepreneur needs to explore ideas, plans, goals, targets and keep track of important stories.

Every mentor I've ever had keeps a journal on them. It shows up at every meeting, it goes on holiday with them, it rides shotgun next to them in the car and sleeps by their bed at night.

There are so many ideas buzzing about in the entrepreneurial brain. When you start paying more attention, brilliant, multimillion dollar ideas can start to come thick and fast – almost like a replacement for the newsfeed.

Ideas need to be explored on paper. Calculations need to be done, resources need to be explored, lists of missing pieces need to be accounted for and diagrams need to be sketched.

No matter how smart you are, you need a journal.

My first mentor, Jon, insisted that I keep a journal. He would give me a magazine and tell me to rewrite the ads in a way that was more customer focused.

He would get me to work out projected revenues on campaigns we were running. He would ask me to list all the goals I wanted to achieve by my next birthday, and make a tally of all the things I was most grateful for to date.

My journals filled up quickly and, by writing these things down, I noticed that my mind was free to have even more ideas.

To this day I'm constantly surprised when I go back through my journals from years earlier. Quite regularly the things I named as 'big goals' were things I could tick off the list just 24 months later.

Get into the habit of writing in your entrepreneur journal. Even if you just sit with it open and make lists of things that come to your mind. If you've not kept a regular journal it can seem foreign to sit and write but, eventually, you wake up a very creative part of your brain that loves to express itself.

Here are some key things to write down to get you started:

What are you most grateful for this month?

Who's been helping you recently whom you haven't acknowledged?

What do you want to achieve before the end of the year?

What frustrations or problems have you noticed people struggling with?

What trends or opportunities are you noticing?

If you had $100k, how would you spend it to grow your business?

Who can you take out to lunch this month who might be a useful contact in the future?

What headlines and hooks would you use to capture attention for your business?

What have you noticed since carrying $1000 in your pocket?

Challenge 8: Plan Inspiring Holidays First

Take out a yearly planner (Go through your yearly planner and put in the holidays you want to take) and put in the holidays you want to take. Blank out the time you'll be taking off in the coming year. Rule out the long weekends you plan on taking and the mid-week lazy days you want off.

When I started working with Jon, he showed me his yearly planner. It was a large poster sized board with all of the days of the year mapped out on it. I noticed big chunks of time boxed out that said things like 'Holiday – Greek Islands' or 'Family Skiing Trip'. Around these holidays, we put in the campaigns and key events we intended to run as a business.

I picked up this approach and have since passed it on to many friends who also swear by it.

This task is an exciting one and it will do wonders for you as an entrepreneur.

Most people plan their holidays around their work. They hope there will be some spare time and money for holidays each year. Holidays aren't a luxury – you are not a robot, you're a human being with limited time to explore the earth – make them a priority.

The successful people I know plan their work around their holidays and so should you.

Start the year by blocking out at least 8 weeks of holiday time. Take out a big year planner at the beginning of the year and block your holidays first. Work out where you want to go, how much you need to set aside and then reverse engineer your work to serve the lifestyle you want to live.

Why is this important? Firstly, it allows your brain to relax about 'getting downtime' because it knows the holidays are coming. This allows you to get so much done when you are working. It also allows your family and friends to relax about when they will be able to spend some real quality time with you. If your family know that there are planned holidays, they won't worry so much if you have to be home late or work through a weekend here and there.

Next, holidays also give you time to think. I have my best ideas on holiday. With some distance between me and the functional elements of my business, I get to play with the big picture and the really important stuff. It's amazing how powerful it is to get some time in nature, away from all the screens. Holidays recharge you.

Finally, your holidays ensure you have deadlines. It's amazing how much gets done the week before you take two weeks to go sailing with limited WiFi. The week before, you somehow move mountains so you can switch off and enjoy the trip.

For most of the last 10 years, I've started the year by blocking out my holidays. There have been a few years where I forgot to do it proactively, and I ended up not taking my holidays.

As a result of this principle, I feel I've had an interesting multidimensional decade. As well as building businesses, I've had some great adventures. I've sailed Thailand, Vanuatu, the Mediterranean and the Australian coast. I've snowboarded the Alps, the Rockies, and in Japan and Australia. I've explored Asia and Indonesia. I've volunteered and raised funds in India and Africa. I've partied in Ibiza, Las Vegas, Bali and Morocco.

The years I took holidays were always much better than the ones I just worked. Better financially, better for my morale, better for connecting with people, better for big dreams and better for my health.

Don't skip this step. Find a way to make it happen.

CHALLENGE 9: GET STRUCTURED

Make an appointment with an accountant and a lawyer to discuss your business and wealth-building plans. Ask them to steer you in the right direction for tax planning, wealth protection and attracting investment.

At age 20, I sat across the table from a business accountant named Matt. We talked about my plans to be an entrepreneur one day and he explained to me how that might look through his eyes. He told me about company structures that would protect me, enable me to become independently valuable and qualify for lower taxes or government grants.

It was a whole new world to discover these non-human entities that had different rights, responsibilities and legal status to me. I started to see how the wealthy use structures to play by a different set of rules than most individuals.

Entrepreneurs learn how the system works so they can legally structure themselves and live exactly how they want. Entrepreneurs believe they should pay the minimum amount of tax legally required of them and not more.

Entrepreneurs believe it would be folly to expose their empire to unnecessary risks or taxes. Entrepreneurs want to create a structure that is attractive to investors, grant-funding opportunities and high-performing employees.

All of this takes planning.

Whether you know it or not, you spend 100% of your life interacting with legal and taxation systems – it's crazy not to understand them.

Most people think they will set up a structure *after* they make a lot of money. Sadly, this doesn't work.

You must create a wealth structure before you make money. It's a nasty catch-22. Companies, trusts, accountants and lawyers all cost money and you have to spend this money before you have it.

Wealth structures are an investment and you need to find ways to build them.

To make matters worse, most lawyers and accountants cannot advise you on ways to avoid paying taxes or avoiding legal obligations – especially after the fact. Technically you have to 'instruct' them what you want to do and they then advise you on the way to carry out your plans.

If you don't know what to ask for, they often won't tell you – it opens them up to risk to do that. For example, if you ask an accountant and a lawyer to tell you how to create a seamless way to pass wealth across generations and open up new options for who pays taxes in what jurisdictions they won't reveal very much. If you tell your accountant that you want to set up a family trust that holds assets like shares in a holding company for your kids, they will talk to you about what that entails – you instructed them.

No one is born with an inbuilt knowledge of how legal and accounting systems operate. It's something you need to learn yourself so that you know what to ask for.

I recommend that you talk to lawyers and accountants before you make a lot of money for the purposes of understanding how things work. Many lawyers and accountants will meet you for an hour, free of charge. Some of them will have lunch with you if you're paying.

To complete this challenge you should set up several meetings with these business advisors to discuss your plans. Even if you don't go ahead with any of their suggestions, you will be more knowledgeable about your options. When you feel ready, you can instruct them to set up a structure that is better for you to build and hold on to more wealth.

Challenge 10: Get Your Entrepreneurial Team in Place

Build a team of people around you who can help you to implement your ideas and achieve the big goals you have for your future. No matter if you are starting out or you're already a millionaire, it will be the team you build today that will determine the results you get tomorrow.

I've been part of dozens of startup ventures and all of the good ones start with a group of people sitting around a table with notepads and laptops, fleshing out a concept. Great businesses don't start with one person doing everything on their own for years at a time, they start by cobbling together small teams.

My first experience of this was with Jon. On day one, he assembled four of us young people around the kitchen bench with him and his wife. We spent the day mapping out a launch campaign, writing advertising copy and phone scripts. We jumped on the phone and spoke to potential suppliers. We debated ways to quickly generate leads and make sales. By the end of the first day, we were aligned and focused on our next 90 days. Despite being an inexperienced team, we were energised and committed.

Until you're able to recruit players onto your team, there's no point running onto the field. Even if your team are rebels and misfits, it's better than trying to achieve anything on your own.

If you currently work for a large company, maybe you aren't ready to be the person who starts a business from scratch. It may be that your best move towards entrepreneurship is to join a small business team that exists or is forming. You'll learn more and earn more working for an experienced entrepreneur first before you take the role of the founder.

I started out as a valuable player on my mentor's team, then I built a team of my own. When I launched my first company I picked a few friends to be around the table with me and kick things off.

Glen was in sales and would earn a commission on each sale. Nick was in operations, in exchange for a free room and food in my house plus a low hourly rate. My cousin Fiona was doing the accounts on Saturday afternoon for a little bit of cash. My girlfriend Kristy had a job but could help out preparing for the launch event. My dad designed our ads and marketing materials. My school friend Kris said he could do 2–3 days setting up some IT systems and we could pay him 'when the business took off'.

I knew it wasn't until I built a team that I was able to start my business.

There's no such thing as a self-made millionaire. In every case, individuals often described as self-made are surrounded by a whole team of people who get things done.

If you are starting out, here's my draft pick for who you should have around the table on day one:

1. A visionary – big picture focused, good at delegating, hardworking and can communicate the vision of the business, make sales and bring in new partnerships (probably you).
2. A design wiz – can take the vision and create brochures, websites, sales forms, business cards, and make a business idea look tangible.
3. A sales gun – someone who's good with people, likable and can ask cheeky questions. This person will either be an appointment setter or a sales closer. If they set

appointments you'll be the one who makes the sale. If they are a sales closer, you'll need a marketing campaign that drops a steady stream of warm leads bookings in their diary.

4. A Swiss army knife – someone who isn't 100% brilliant in any one thing, but can get most things done well enough. They are organised, flexible, frugal and detail orientated. They can do data entry if required, customer service calls, order supplies, book flights, fix most IT problems or quickly find someone who can.

5. A mentor – outside the business, successful, wise, been around the block and had a few bloody noses, available for late-night chats over a glass of wine. This could also take the form of a mastermind group rather than just one person.

In the early days, these people don't need to be full-time employees. They could be on an hourly or weekly arrangement. They could be on commission or even just helping you out because they're interested in seeing the project launch.

Early stage businesses don't typically hire A-players. They get going with a rag-tag group of rebels and misfits. My first businesses started with people who had no experience or qualifications, we just figured things out and had fun together solving problems. At a later date, the proper employees show up and bring with them the proper ways of doing things.

If you're already in business, with an existing team, you can still apply this strategy. Set up a skunk-works team to develop a new product or marketing campaign. Rope in some people from your network to attend some meetings and discuss ways to transform the business you have into the business of your dreams.

Some of the best entrepreneurs I know are quite bad at putting business plans together, and tend to write notes on scraps of paper more often than they write detailed plans. One thing they are good at, however, is recruiting the right people around them and building a culture where high performers want to stay.

Entrepreneurial teams don't start with a plan, they create one together. Then they get to work. They get sales in the door, keep customers happy, keep costs down, start early, finish late, communicate powerfully and stand strong under pressure.

Make a list of people to enrol onto your entrepreneurial team. Start keeping an eye out for a great sales person, a detail-oriented administrator, a customer service person, and so on.

You simply can't build a successful business on your own. You need to become a master at spotting the potential in everyone you meet.

Don't Skip the Tough Challenges

The tasks that I set out each have hidden lessons built in. Each task is designed to awaken your inner entrepreneur and remove your fears about building a business.

If any of these tasks really challenge you and you feel uncomfortable, try to dig deep and look for the underlying beliefs that make it so challenging. Over the years, I have seen these ten challenges bring up some strange beliefs in my clients.

What might you believe about money that prevents you from carrying it?

If you worry that you will lose it, explore why you feel you are irresponsible with money. If you are scared of being mugged, take a look at your belief that having money means attracting bad people and events.

What do you believe about yourself that stops you from associating only with inspirational people?

If you are worried that they won't like you, what makes you feel so unworthy? If you are afraid they will take advantage of you, explore why you believe successful people are manipulative.

What is it that makes you feel so uneasy about switching off from news, taking leaps into the unknown or planning great holidays?

Anything at all that comes up in your mind and stops you from implementing these ideas is worth taking a good look at.

Is it possible these limiting beliefs are holding you back in other areas of your life too? If so, you need to push through and do the toughest tasks first.

I promise you these ten challenges will change your life, if you are willing to trust the process.

It's not easy going from the world of 'industrialized factory worker' to the world of 'entrepreneurial adventurer'.

Society has so many unspoken rules about what you should and shouldn't be doing. These ten challenges will most definitely feel uncomfortable at first because they deliberately rub up against these old rules.

I've given you ten ways to tunnel out of the confines of the Industrial Revolution and into the freedom of the Entrepreneur Revolution. Take your time, keep digging and inch by inch you will be closer to a whole new level of freedom.

You don't need to start your entrepreneurial journey by starting a business. Most successful entrepreneurs I talk to about how they got started go back to an early mentor, a small campaign to sell something, a sales job or working alongside a founder. It's typical that they built their confidence with small steps before starting a business of their own.

Everyone has a comfort zone that holds them back from getting what they want. Get a coach, a mentor or join a group to hold you accountable if you need to, but push yourself to get the breakthrough you want.

Each step you take will give you experience, a mindset shift and access to more resources. There will come a point when you are totally ready to start your business; you will know that it's time to follow your heart.

Case Study: Getting Started

Sarah used to work for a large corporation. Each morning she would scan her badge, make her way up the elevator to spend time completing tasks and having meetings. The company was so big she had no idea what the bigger picture was, she just knew what her division was responsible for and that she played an important role in 'making the future brighter through software and data analytics', which is what it said on the glass wall of the shared area in her office.

Sarah started dreaming of starting a business. It looked amazing on Instagram; people her age boarding planes to Dubai, taking clients to dinner in fancy restaurants and doing Zoom meetings from a colourful beanbag and doing wellness days for the dynamic little team.

Making the jump from a big company to a complete standing start seemed impossible though and a year went by without any progress towards her goal. Then one day she heard about a small startup business that was hiring for a role running marketing campaigns. The business only had a team of six people and was only a year old. Sarah got the job and joined the startup as employee number seven.

The role was nothing like she imagined. She was doing all sorts of things like sales calls, customer support, procurement, research and supplier briefing. No two weeks were the same and the small business was completely transparent about everything. It was normal to overhear conversations about revenue numbers, profit and even mistakes that had been made.

The founder often went to coffee with Sarah and they discussed business strategy, random ideas and stressful issues that come up. Sarah's mindset towards business shifted too. She realised that she had been naive when it came to her expectations of what a startup would be like.

The startup didn't have an IT department to help log into a secure portal. There was no learning and development manager to request training from. Taking a holiday felt guilty because there was no one to cover her role. The cash reserves of the business always seemed dangerously low and a few expensive mistakes would make the founder stressed out and emotional. The company Instagram account looked amazing – but the reality was a lot more stressful and demanding than people would guess.

After two years of this work, Sarah felt ready to start a business. She had helped grow the small startup to over 40 employees and she understood the playbooks that got through the tough times. She approached the founder of the business and pitched her idea for a startup. To her surprise, she was offered her first amount of seed funding and the blessing of her employer.

Sarah launched her business with two people supporting her launch event. She had grown so much from her experience working for a startup and going out on her own didn't feel scary anymore. Her launch campaign was a hit and she shifted straight into growth mode hiring another two people in the first six months. She knew that entrepreneurship wasn't always as shiny as the Instagram posts but it was the path she wanted to be on and she was inspired to be building her dream.

CHAPTER 4

FINDING YOUR OPPORTUNITY

Having woken up your entrepreneurial brain, you are now ready to find an entrepreneurial opportunity. This requires you to conduct four experiments that I call CAOS – concept, audience, offer and sales:

Concept – you must choose an idea to work on and test to see if people respond favourably to the broad strokes of the idea.

Audience – you choose a target customer and test if you are able to capture their attention.

Offer – you must present potential customers with something they can buy to achieve an outcome and then ask what they like or don't like about it.

Sales – you must discover a predictable and repeatable way to make enough sales for your business to survive.

1. Concept – The Entrepreneur Sweet Spot

In these exciting times we're living in, for the first time in history, it's easy to make an income from almost anything you want if you create a global small business around it. A great concept is found at your 'entrepreneur sweet spot'.

1. Something you're passionate about.
2. Something that solves a problem.
3. Something that makes money.

Two out of three is not enough. If you are passionately solving meaningful problems but you aren't earning money, you'll feel unrewarded and resentful. If you earn money solving important problems but you lack passion you will get distracted and exit as soon as you can afford to. If you make money and you enjoy what you do but you aren't solving a meaningful problem, you will start to feel unethical and purposeless. When you combine all three you will be fulfilled, rewarded and energised by what you do. You'll get good at it, stick with it and your results will compound.

Let's address these aspects one at a time.

Discovering Your Passion

Passionate people have a huge advantage over dispassionate people. A passionate person attracts opportunities like a magnet.

Vidal Sassoon was the world's highest paid hairdresser ever; he built an empire on his passion. Here's how he describes his job:

> How fortuitous to be able to touch the human frame. To be exhilarated by a craft that constantly changes; to hold that substance growing from a human form that moulds, creates spontaneous fashion. To be involved in the poetry of change.

Apparently, he's talking about cutting hair! He could only speak this way out of a genuine love of his craft.

Many people struggle with the big question 'what's my purpose?' or 'what should I do that I'm passionate about?'

It might seem like a big question, but it's actually not that hard to discover if you know the right questions to ask so you can tune into the passion that's already present.

After discussing this topic with hundreds of entrepreneurs I believe a theme has been present for most of your life already. Whether you are conscious of it or not, there's an underlying theme of passion since you were a child.

For me, the theme is solving meaningful problems with entrepreneurship, conducting intensely focused campaigns to engage people and fundraising for charity. For as long as I can remember, the big moments in my life revolved around these themes.

At age 10, I was running garage sales from my parents' house. I wouldn't just sell our family unwanted items, I would sell the neighbours' stuff on consignment as well.

As a kid, I was washing cars and pulling weeds to raise money for my Scout hall. As a teenager, I was running dance parties at the school to raise money for causes.

At the intersection of these themes I find myself incredibly passionate even to this day.

Today, I have multiple businesses focused on serving entrepreneurs. I raise money for charities through business and running powerful campaigns.

When someone offers me an opportunity, I simply need to decide if it fits with these themes of solving meaningful problems through entrepreneurship and high-impact campaigns.

Your life also has a theme. There are things you've been doing almost your whole life that you keep coming back to. The trick is to discover what that theme is.

Your theme will probably combine two or three ingredients. Oprah's theme combines mass media with a daily dose of inspiration. When those things come together she gets her spark and things grow effortlessly.

Most people tell me that their history contains many unrelated activities. After probing deeply with hundreds of people on this topic I know this isn't the case. I know that all the things that genuinely excite a person are connected.

Richard Branson has 150 companies in the Virgin empire. At first glance it would seem that they are all unrelated – what does an airline have to do with credit cards or mobile phones?

Probe a little deeper and you'll see that there's a theme. Richard Branson loves to shake up stale industries, champion underdogs and make work fun. He did it with magazines, music stores, airlines and banks – along with dozens of other industries that took themselves too seriously. If he sticks to the theme, he's happy and his businesses work.

I describe it like an apple tree. There might be lots of separate apples on the tree, but there's just one tree that keeps growing them. Likewise, there might be a lot of opportunities that interest you, but there's one key theme that links them together.

To get more apples, you need a big, strong apple tree. To get more of the right opportunities you need to understand what your theme is.

ACTIVITY: DISCOVER YOUR 'THEME'

Your 'theme' will take the form of a rant that begins with any of these four sentences.

1. 'For as long as I can remember I've felt there's something exciting at the intersection of ... and ...'
2. 'I've always believed the world needs more ... and less ...'

3. 'A long time ago I noticed the power of . . . and . . . . mixed together'
4. 'My whole life I've been fascinated by what happens when you bring together . . . and . . .'

This rant will light you up and excite you. It will feel like a rant that's been waiting to emerge since you were very young. It will feel a bit like a crusade you want to embark on and you don't really care how it happens as long as it unfolds.

This rant is not commercial. It's not 'I believe there needs to be another accountant in London.'

My rant goes like this . . .

I believe there's great power when entrepreneurs focus on solving big social or environmental problems. Entrepreneurship is a vehicle to reclaim power – economically, intellectually, emotionally and spiritually. I believe that an entrepreneurial population is an empowered population and that entrepreneurs, by nature, want to fix the problems that humanity faces. I believe that by creating millions more empowered entrepreneurs we will transform the planet and create a world that works for more people.

None of it is commercial, it's about tapping into a passion that is deeper than any one idea.

With that passion in mind, you want to start looking at the problems in the world that you could solve. The world has plenty of problems that need solving, which is why you start with your passion as a compass to steer you towards the problems that are meant for you to address.

SOLVING A PROBLEM

The next step in moving to the entrepreneur sweet spot is solving a problem.

You can't just be passionate, you also need to deliver real value.

At the heart of every great business concept is something of value that solves a problem for the customer. You cannot build a business if you aren't solving a real problem for people.

No matter how good your sales people are, no matter how much advertising you do, no matter how much you push, if there's no problem being solved there's no business.

I see many entrepreneurs wanting to copy a successful business they admire. By definition, if a business exists that is doing a great job of solving a problem, then the problem is already solved and there's no need to start another one. If there is already an amazing coffee shop on your street and it has plenty of capacity to serve more people, you'd be crazy to start another coffee shop.

What you are looking for is an unmet need. You want to find people who want something that doesn't yet exist. They have a desire that is unfulfilled and your business will fix that for them.

If you notice that there are no coffee shops within 5 miles, you might want to start one.

Problems can be solved better, faster and cheaper. Problems can be solved with more emotional benefits. Jay Shetty noticed that many people felt stressed, anxious, lonely or overwhelmed in the modern world so he started sharing ancient monk wisdom on social media and gave people strategies and inspiration to get back in control of their feelings and relationships. As a result of helping people solve this problem he has a massive business.

You need to look deeper at the problems you have the power to solve. This approach, method or intellectual property will form an important part of your concept.

DISCOVERING YOUR APPROACH TO PROBLEM SOLVING

In business the problem-solving recipe you have is called 'intellectual property', or IP for short.

I'm not necessarily talking about the legal definition of IP that has been formalised with trademarks, patents, and so on. I'm talking about your unique approach to solving a problem better, cheaper, faster and with more emotional benefits than others.

Intellectual property represents your method of doing something, your unique philosophy behind what you do, the recipes for success that you know.

Your business will have products, services, media and content available. All of these things are infused with magical stuff called IP.

So how do you create more of it? How do you know what IP you already have but take for granted? How do you dig up this gold?

You write.

You write articles, you write books, you write brochures, you write a thesis, you add diagrams and you get what's in your head and into a document.

Most of the IP you have goes swirling through your brain so fast that you call it 'intuition'. When you write, you will discover that it's not intuitive. It's a thought process that happens really quickly.

Only when you sit down and write about what you do will you be able to slow it down enough to see what's really going on.

Whenever I have an idea, my first step is to write about it. I will write a blog or create a brochure for it. In doing so, I need to pin the idea down and make sure there's real value in it. When I see the blog or the brochure it either feels real or it becomes obvious how many ingredients are missing.

I also write case studies about clients we've helped. It makes me slow down and deconstruct the elements that were behind the success story.

In writing books, I become much clearer on many aspects of my personal philosophy, my methods and my value. I've talked a lot about these ideas but something magic happens when I have to write them down.

The content that you write will be used to make products, marketing materials, employee handbooks, investor memorandums and websites. Writing it down makes it scalable.

People will read what you write and decide if they want to spend time with you, buy from you, partner with you and even invest in you. Rarely can people make the decision to do any of that unless they read something. Certainly, it's hard to scale your business without great written content.

If you've never written much before, don't worry. You aren't trying to win a literary award; you're trying to slow down your mind and access valuable ideas.

ACTIVITY: DISCOVER YOUR 'IP'

Start by thinking of a time when you added value to someone. You solved a problem, they thanked you and you either got paid for it or they would have happily paid for the result. Now write about it.

Write the story of what the problem was and how you understood the deeper nature of the problem. Write about the steps you took to solve it. Write about the positive impact of solving the problem in the longer term. Add some research to your writing – data, statistics, academic studies.

Next, write some blogs or articles that explore this in different ways. Here's a list of things to write about relating to your topic:

Seven mistakes people make while trying to achieve a result.

Five valuable ideas more people should be aware of if they want to solve the problem.

Ten maxims to live by if you want to avoid the problem.

Five things that stop people implementing good ideas and getting better results.

Three case studies of success stories.

Trust the process. Sit down and write your ideas down. You will discover that you are standing on mountains of intellectual property you take for granted.

When you examine successful people, a common trait is they write a lot. They keep journals, they publish articles and write papers. They are often authors of books.

This isn't just for the people reading it; it's for the author too. They develop valuable IP as a result of the writing process. You will develop valuable IP if you write too.

The next step is commercialising your ideas. If you want to make real money from your intellectual property, read on.

MAKING MONEY

The third step to living in the entrepreneur sweet spot is to earn great money.

In the Entrepreneur Revolution, you don't need to become a billionaire to be successful. In the past, business was hard and didn't necessarily relate to a passion. If you went travelling, business suffered. If you wanted to scale up, you had to sacrifice time with friends and family. Solving problems was expensive, dangerous or arduous. The reward for being able to endure the suffering of running a business was money.

The entrepreneur revolution is different by design because we can make money doing things we would enjoy doing anyway. Our global small businesses can expand when we travel and have fun, they can make money when we are talking passionately or sharing our ideas on a big platform. We can solve problems at a massive scale using technology that is free or almost free.

There's been extensive research into the link between money and happiness. Statistically, money does make you happier. Up to a point.

Once you earn an amount that allows you to be comfortable, it matters more to your happiness how you make your money.

The social media has people convinced that they need to be making millions to be fulfilled. On Instagram happiness requires six cars, four houses, a treasure chest full of jewellery and endless travel.

Supposedly, we're meant to make all this money while we sleep and doing something that causes no stress.

As a result of this fantasy, I regularly see people who write down goals of millions (sometimes even billions) as their financial targets for achieving happiness. This is a surefire recipe to be incredibly disappointed for the rest of your life.

For most people, you don't need to build a massive business and earn millions in order to be living in the Entrepreneur Revolution. You can build a lifestyle business that generates a healthy income, by doing what you are passionate about. That allows you to take home a healthy income while still having a great deal of freedom and lifestyle.

Some of the happiest entrepreneurs I know have a small team, selling a niche offering to an engaged community of people from around the world. Ali Abdaal is a YouTuber in London. He makes videos and courses about productivity and has a book called *Feel Good Productivity*. His team of 10 make millions in revenue from YouTube, courses and book sales. He doesn't need to exit for billions to be happy – he's living in his entrepreneur sweet spot.

You need to reverse-engineer the financial future that inspires you. Start with the amount you want in order to live the lifestyle you desire. When you have your number, you must discover how many customers you need in order to hit that target and perhaps go beyond it.

FORECASTING YOUR FUTURE

A financial forecast is a crystal ball that tells you the future of your business. It typically takes the form of a spreadsheet that looks at the sales you plan on making minus the costs associated with making those sales and running your business.

At this early stage you only need a forecast that is directionally correct. You don't yet know exactly what you will be selling or how much everything will cost but there are basic assumptions you can start looking at and as you collect more information you can plug it into this spreadsheet.

A few key decisions will determine how much money you can make.

There's the type of customer you are going to serve. Some people solve problems by throwing money at them while other people are more frugal and would rather put their own time to work instead of parting with cash. As a general rule, if you serve a market that is affluent and happy to spend in order to get the result they want, it's far easier to build a business. I have seen many upset entrepreneurs who seem surprised that they didn't make much money with an offer aimed at broke students. I've also seen many entrepreneurs who sell something to large corporations and make excellent money serving a small number of clients who have big budgets they have to get through.

As a general rule, selling to a business is much better than selling to individual consumers. A business typically has much more money to spend and is incentivised to spend money on improving rather than paying taxes on profit. When you calculate the 'lifetime value' (LTV) of a customer it will typically be much higher if you are selling to a business.

Finding a type of customer who has money to spend is a great clue that your business will succeed in the short term. If you discover there are many of these people or businesses in the world you have the potential to grow and grow for years. It's worth doing some digging into how many buyers might be out there in your 'total addressable market' (TAM).

When you have calculated how big your market is, you want to look at what percentage of the 'market share' your business would need to sell to in order for you to hit your dream lifestyle. A great business opportunity is one where you've found buyers who have money to spend; there are plenty of them out there and you only need to sell to a tiny number of them in order for your business to succeed.

Looking at your lifetime value of a customer, the total addressable market and the market share is a great place to start when deciding if your business will make money.

Constructing a basic financial forecast for your business will then tell you how hard it will be to hit your life-style goals.

2. Audience – Capturing the Attention of Your Customers

With an exciting concept, you need to test that you are able to build an audience who are invested in what you are up to. An audience is different to a market. A market is the number of people who theoretically might buy something but an audience consists of people who are paying attention to what you are doing.

The market size is mostly irrelevant to an entrepreneur.

Some new and innovative ideas have tiny markets to begin with – there was no PC market in 1977 when Apple launched, there was no market for user-generated videos before YouTube and there was no market for renting a bedroom in a stranger's house before AirBnB.

Some markets are huge but it's very unlikely you will successfully enter them. It's unlikely that you will successfully launch a new luxury watch brand or a burger restaurant chain. Yes there's a big market and there's still ways to improve things but the effort required to enter these markets and make a splash would be enormous.

What matters more than the market size is the audience – people who stop what they are doing and want to know more about what you are doing. The great news is you can build an audience before you have a product or a service to sell. In fact, that is exactly what you should do.

When Elon Musk decided to launch a futuristic electric pickup truck he didn't build the factory and produce the cars in secret. Instead, he tested to see if he could build an audience who were interested in the CyberTruck by hosting an event and getting millions of people to join his audience.

He stood on the stage, showed people the prototype and the planned specification. He shared the story of why he wanted to create this product and who it was created for. He then said that it would be years before this product would be ready. But, you could put down a holding deposit of $100 if you wanted to reserve one on the priority list.

Over one million people put down a holding deposit, totalling over $100 million of deposit money. The money wasn't the valuable part though; he was able to use the waiting list as proof that his latest product was a hit. With such a strong vote of confidence from his audience he was able to get all the funding he needed to build the factory to fulfil the orders.

Most struggling entrepreneurs don't do this. Instead they slave away in secret, building all the things they will need in order to deliver the scalable solution they imagine people want. Only too late do they discover that despite having a brilliantly engineered product, no one is even remotely interested. They could have discovered this with a few fast and easy tests.

SIGNALS FIRST, THEN BUILD

Before you launch anything, you need a signal from your audience that they want to proceed. You will need to give

your audience enough information for them to get the gist
of what you are creating but you don't need to give them
absolutely every detail. It's wise to have slides, simple designs
and some basic marketing materials available so people don't
need to read your mind – but don't overdo it.

There are four campaigns I recommend that will give
you a signal of interest:

1. A waiting list – ask people to join a priority waiting list
   for your new business, product or innovation. Let them
   know that people on the list will be given updates when
   they are available and will be invited to see, test or access
   the product before anyone else.
2. An online discussion group – invite people to join a
   group you host on a social media platform or discussion
   app like WhatsApp. Let people know that you are going
   to be sharing relevant book recommendations, videos
   and podcasts relating to the topic of your business. For
   example, if you are launching a fitness-related business,
   you launch a fitness discussion group.
3. An introduction event – host an online event that
   introduces people to key ideas that relate to your new
   business idea. This should be a short presentation of
   30–60 minutes that allows you to present some of the
   insights you think people should be aware of that tighten
   their interest in your new business. If you are launching
   a web development agency, invite people to an event on
   Zoom where you look at five high-performing websites
   and you showcase what they are doing differently. That

information will likely make people feel inclined to think about updating their website.

4. An online assessment or quiz – people love to complete questionnaires if it leads to something of value for them. Correctly set up (like on ScoreApp.com), these online assessments are a magnet for collecting interest and information about your potential buyers. A simple but effective quiz concept is a scorecard that tells someone if they are suitable or ready to make some sort of change – for example: Are you ready to run a marathon? Answer 10 questions and find out.

Using these four methods, you want to build an audience that is significantly large enough to hit your sales targets. Typically only 1 in 20 people in your audience will buy something right away so if you want to be sure that you will make plenty of sales, you need your audience size to exceed 200 people for every 10 sales you want to make when you launch. It never hurts to have plenty of people ready to go.

FIND THE PEOPLE WITH THE MONEY

Inside your audience you will start to see a few groups emerging. Some people will love what you do but do not have any money to spend – often these people represent the majority of people in your audience. You'll also spot people who are interested in what you do and they can spend money if they want. If you are lucky, you might also discover a small minority of people who want what you have to offer and money is no object for them. These people are likely to be a tiny minority but often they have the budget to make up for it.

Ignore the larger crowd with no money to begin with. Go and talk to the people with the money and discover what they need to know in order to buy. You are looking for the people who have reasonable expectations and can justify spending money on what you offer. If you look after these people they will be happy and will refer you to more people like themselves.

There's an old joke about working with clients and their expectations. It compares the experience of a photographer who agrees to shoot a budget wedding and gets 100 demands from the bride and groom, with that of a corporate event planner who simply pays the big budget invoice and sends a text 'Great pics. Thx.' It lampoons the common trope that customers with a small budget typically have more demands than customers with big budgets.

Remember that you are not your buyer. Starting a new business, you might be worried about spending even small amounts of money. For you, money might be an emotional topic and you would never entertain throwing money at a problem. A corporate buyer is wired completely the opposite way. For them it's not their money and they have no emotion about spending it. They want a problem solved as best as it can be so they don't look bad in front of their peers. They'd feel better spending more money and feeling sure that it won't reflect badly on them.

Money is relative. A Ferrari is an expensive car to a schoolteacher, it's a toy to a billionaire, it's capital expenditure to a luxury car rental business and it will make a profit. The most expensive couples therapist in the world is Esther Perel. Her fees are astronomical to most people but to someone who's worth $100 million, if she can prevent a costly divorce, she's cheap. Be sure you are talking to people who have money and can see the value in what you do for them.

OFFER – SHOWING PEOPLE THE VALUE YOU CAN DELIVER

Building a significant audience gives you the confidence that there are people ready to spend money to achieve an outcome or solve a problem if you give them a great offer. A compelling offer is one that addresses all of people's needs and wants and removes as much risk as possible.

The schooling system does not teach kids how to create a compelling offer – it does the opposite. At school we are guided towards developing a set of skills that we can then plug in to an established organisation. This model of employment treats you as the component labour that someone else will use to make their business run. You don't need to know what the business does or how much it makes, you just need to show up and do your little bit and you will get paid your wage.

When most people go out to start a business they do what the school system taught them to do – they sell their labour. If they have web design skills they start a business building websites and they spend all day using their skills. If they are trained up as a lawyer, they go off and become a self-employed lawyer working with their customers on legal issues. This self-employed approach is not entrepreneurship.

An entrepreneur starts by looking closely at a customer's wants and needs. They probe to discover what the customer sees as less than perfect about their current situation. They ask the customer about their hopes, dreams and aspirations. They work to understand what obstacles the customer has encountered while trying to get what they want.

Armed with all of this information, the entrepreneur starts constructing a list of things that would deliver the outcome the customer wants. They package everything up and present it back to the customer as one, simple, packed up thing that a customer can easily buy. This is their offer.

Consider the iPhone. It appears to be one thing but it's far from it. There are 18 major suppliers Apple needs to build the iPhone and there are at least 200 additional second-tier suppliers who make parts, move things around, package, design, process or test along the way. The box it comes in, the cables, the glass, the steel, the chips and the batteries are all made by companies that aren't Apple. You might even be surprised to discover that Apple's main rival – Samsung – is a major supplier of parts to Apple.

What about your local pizza restaurant – they have a special deal for pizza and wine but how much of it do they do? The ingredients come from all over the world, the wine comes from a vineyard, their physical restaurant is leased, they buy candles from a wholesaler, their tablecloths are washed and returned by another company and the list goes on and on.

Both Apple and the pizza restaurant have packaged up ingredients that give the customer what they want. This collection of ingredients is presented to a customer as one thing. The customer buys the iPhone or the romantic candlelit dinner without any awareness of all the components that went into the mix.

BUILD THE BROCHURE

An offer comes into existence when the customer can clearly see what they can buy. In most cases the marketing materials show the customer what the offer includes. It is often the case that a person will see the brochure for the thing they want and then order it. Once they order it, the business will do what needs to be done to deliver it. It was the brochure that gave someone what they needed to know in order to buy. I recommend you build the brochure before you do anything expensive or time consuming.

Here's how to build the brochure:

1. Understand the desire: I recommend getting 150 people in your audience to complete a survey and then talking to at least 30 of them. You want to understand what they want, what they struggle with and what they are frustrated by currently. You want to know what they have tried previously and what their budget is for solving their problem. Look for recurring themes that everyone seems to mention.

2. Build a specifications list: compile all of the key ingredients into a list of features. Package in all the things they want or need, not just the things you know how to do. For example, you might include a book you want them to read, some software you think they should use or some training they require – all of this could be from other providers.

3. Go back and check – create some basic diagrams and images that you can show and return to 10–30 people and get feedback on what they think about the basic specifications and designs. Don't feel bad that you are wasting your time or theirs, this process is actually quite fun for people and it can heighten their desire to buy from you when the package is ready.

4. Create the brochure – give your package a name and write 500–1500 words of content about it. Talk about how it was created and why. Discuss the desired outcomes it provides. Describe who it is for and the problems it solves. Ideally use AI or a copywriter to help you write compelling copy. Then hand it over to a designer who can create a great-looking version of your brochure. When it's ready, print out 50 physical copies that you can show customers in addition to the digital version.

A brochure is a powerful sales tool and, unlike a website, it is something you can use while talking to real customers face to face or on a call. Eventually you'll put all of the brochure content on a website but for now a brochure is all you need. A brochure is all you need to present customers with an offer.

If you are launching something really innovative, you don't need to know how you will actually make your offer in reality. If you want to sell tickets to a moon-base hotel, create a brochure and see how customers react. If someone wants to pay you millions for a ticket you might instead put them in a VIP waiting list. If you do take a payment for a product you haven't yet secured, be sure to put the money aside so you can give them a refund if you cannot materialise what you envisioned.

Property developers sell building that don't exist with a brochure. Technology companies sell gadgets that don't exist with brochures. Event promoters sell tickets to shows that are 6 months in the future using a brochure. Whatever it is you want to launch, get the brochure first and see how it sells.

SALES – PREDICTABLY GETTING CUSTOMERS TO BUY

It's a good thing to get a few people joining a waiting list or putting down a deposit but pretty quickly you need to establish a way of predictably and reliably making sales.

As a consumer of products, you rarely come into contact with a sales person. Most products that are priced for consumers don't require a sales person and most established brands have figured out ways to sell things online rather than face to face.

It may come as a shock to you that almost every new business requires the founder to make sales – normally face to face. You might have reservations about making sales. You might think that if a product is good enough it will sell itself or that sales is somehow a process of manipulation. You will have to put aside all of these beliefs so you can get your business off the ground by making sales.

Even tech companies with an online product offer start with sales meetings. When I launched ScoreApp, I sat face to face with well over 1000 business owners and sold the software solution we had developed. The 'sale' was to take a 30-day free trial and then subscribe for $39 per month (with the ability to cancel at any time).

At this time in my career, my time was worth thousands of dollars per hour as a keynote speaker or high-end consultant but I decided it was worth it for me to be on the front line talking to customers at the moment they were making a decision about my offer.

The sales meetings gave me the exact language to use to explain the value proposition of ScoreApp. During those meetings I found the right examples, analogies, stories and statistics to build a compelling case for my product. I also found objections and resistance from customers that lead to making product changes. None of this would have happened if I had just put up a website and tried to observe my customers from a safe distance.

Most services businesses are sales businesses. A new photographer imagines herself at weddings taking gorgeous photos of the bridal party but rarely thinks about the hundreds of sales meetings she must do in order to win the paid work in the first place. Customers have choices and they want to talk to suppliers before they settle on a decision. These are sales presentations.

The biggest and most luxurious brands in the world are all masters at professional sales conversations. Rolex has a bootcamp that all sales people go through regularly. LVMH has approved sales trainers who work with retail employees on the best ways to sell their handbags and fashion items. Tesla, BMW, Bentley and Range Rover all rely upon highly trained sales people to hit their targets. Salesforce is a software provider to the world's biggest companies who use the tools to make their armies of salespeople more effective.

If the world's biggest brands have sales people and a professional sales approach, you will not be able to avoid this part of your business at any scale. Whether it's selling your startup to Angel Investors, signing up the first 500 subscribers of your software or landing that whale of a client your business needs, as the founder of a business, you are the one who will need to lead the charge.

THE RHYTHM OF SUCCESS

Mastering sales isn't about having a great campaign or delivering a perfect presentation once or twice. Successful sales results happen when you get into a repeatable rhythm every week. I have grown dozens of businesses, mostly starting from scratch, and one of the first things we put in place is the 'Weekly LAPS Dashboard'. This LAPS dashboard measures four stages in a sales pipeline:

Leads – a lead is anyone who you or your sales team should be reaching out and talking to. Ideally a lead is someone who has signalled interest in what you are doing.

They might have joined your waiting list, attended your event or filled in your online scorecard. It might even be a softer signal of interest such as commenting on a social media post or responding to a direct message. As soon as someone starts signalling their interest even in a small way, you must add this person's details to your leads list.

Appointments – once you have a leads list, your next goal is to get people to agree to talk to you by setting an appointment time. They might book into your diary for a one-to-one conversation or they might book into a group presentation or event. They key is to get people to commit to spending some time exploring what you do. If you can't get someone to book an appointment, it's unlikely you will get them to buy your product so the first 'sale' is a commitment of time.

Presentations – when you are in front of a warm prospect, you will need to conduct a sales presentation that shows what you are offering and why it is valuable to them. Your presentation should identify the problem your product solves and highlight the features, advantages and benefits of your particular approach to solving the problem. Every presentation should include a proposal where you present the terms of your offer – the specifications, price, guarantee and any other terms and conditions of the sale. Your presentation should conclude by clearly asking your prospect how they wish to proceed – it should not be ambiguous that you want them to sign up and become a customer.

Sales – when you ask a prospect if they are willing to proceed, they have a few choices. They can flat out reject you, they can agree to go ahead, they can raise objections or ask for more information. Your job as a sales person is to be prepared for any of these situations so you can maximise the number of sales you get each week. From a customer's perspective, their biggest fear is telling you they are not at all interested and you relentlessly pursue them – this rarely happens in reality (and if someone flat out rejects you, it's normally worth moving on to someone else). Most customers who don't say yes right away simply have some questions or a few obstacles that need to be removed before they can proceed. This is where your sales skills and preparation make all the difference.

Your weekly LAPS dashboard tracks the number of leads you generate each week, the appointments you book, the presentations you deliver and the sales you secure. It allows you to discover your baseline numbers and then make adjustments to improve your results.

OPTIMISING THE PIPELINE

I can't think of any one thing I've ever done that has made a radical improvement to my sales pipeline. It's always a series of small things that all add up to a better result. You might discover that you can generate slightly more leads on social media posts if you add a call-to-action at the end. You might discover that people are slightly more likely to book an appointment if you send them a calendar link rather than suggesting a time. You might discover that your presentations go better if you keep them under 45 minutes rather than if they spill over to an hour. You might find that adding a guarantee or a payment plan gives you an edge in your sales results.

Rather than looking for the silver bullet that fixes everything, make a list of three things you could improve for each of the four stages in your sales pipeline. Make the adjustments and then look at the results and see if they helped or hindered you.

Suspend your expectations about how customers behave in the real world. I am frequently shocked at how customers respond, and not in a good way. I have crafted offers that I feel are a total no brainer and they barely shift the results. I remember presenting to a group of 40 perfect potential clients – I presented them with the most elegant solution to the problem they explicitly wanted solved, I gave them a free trial period, a guarantee and the ability to get free support indefinitely until they got the result they wanted. All of this was at a price that was affordable and a fraction of the tangible value of the result they wanted. Out of 40 people, only 12 took me up on the free trial period and only 8 became clients.

When I followed up with the people who didn't take the free trial the most common answer I got was 'I'm sick of subscriptions – I just don't want to buy ANYTHING or spend ANY time setting something up.' This is mind-blowing; they are happy to attend a presentation to address a problem they have but when presented with the perfect solution in a risk free offer, they still won't buy because they don't want to spend any time or any money solving the problem.

No matter what you do, you simply cannot please everyone. For this reason, you are going to need a lot more leads than you probably think, even after you have optimised your sales pipeline. I have access to a lot of data across many industries and the most common conversion of leads to sales is under 5% – even with a solid offer and a well-oiled sales machine. For every sale you want to make, you'll probably need over 20 warm leads. Yep, it's common that 19 out of 20 who signal interest will not purchase what you are offering. Entrepreneurs who accept this harsh reality will succeed and entrepreneurs who have expectations that don't match up to customer behaviour will struggle.

The good news is that to get a business off the ground really only requires CAOS – a sensible Concept, an engaged Audience, an attractive Offer and a diligent Sales approach. These things don't cost a lot of money, they require creative energy. If you get these four things in place, you will have the foundations of a successful business that delivers value and has the potential to be profitable.

CHAPTER 5

BUILDING YOUR GLOBAL SMALL BUSINESS

B usinesses start out as a series of experiments. You are testing to see if you can create something that the market wants and if you have sufficient passion to ride the inevitable bumps and delays that any business will provide in ample abundance.

The COAS method in the previous chapter was about conducting a series of experiments that give you the green lights to build a business that will eventually take on a life of its own. You have found a good concept, you have attracted the attention of an audience, offered them something they want and made consistent sales. Now it's time to start building up your business with a product ecosystem and a core team.

BUILD YOUR MODEL FIRST

An important next step in creating a stable, profitable business is to establish your model. A model shows what you are trying to build. It shows the products and services you will be

offering, the prices you will charge and the revenue streams
you will attract. It also looks at the costs and investments you
need to make in order to sustain those revenues. Your goal is
to build a model that shows how it will scale up over time to
become a profitable, strong and successful business.

If you have ever visited a property developer's office you
will see a model for their property development. It's a sim-
plified little version of what the building and the development site is meant to look like when it's done. At a glance,
people can look at the model and see that the block of dirt
that is there right now will end up with a 15-story residen-
tial building, an underground parking garage, a tennis court,
three swimming pools and four retail stores on ground level.
The model shows the end result but it also shows the construction time and the key stages of the development – it
has the successful end point and the plan to get there.

A property developer would never just start building on
the site and see what happens. They would never tell people
to invest in the project not knowing if it's a house, a building, a warehouse or a farm that their cash is going into. They
wouldn't expect their works to be productive if they had no
idea what the end result was meant to look like. Everyone
who is involved in the project needs to see the model so they
understand what success looks like.

Entrepreneurs need to build a model too. The entrepreneur should create a successful end-point and a plan to get to
that point. Of course the business will continue to trade and
grow past that point but it's important to have a clear target
that you are trying to reverse engineer. When you get there,
you can create a new model for the next stage of development.

A model for an entrepreneur should include two key documents:

Financial forecast – this is a spreadsheet that looks at the income and the expenses month after month into the future. Typically the forecast will be for a period of 24–60 months. This spreadsheet will show how much the business loses or profits each month and you'll know how much money needs to be invested into this business so it doesn't run out of money along the way.

Business plan – this covers the reasons why this business is a good idea for you and your team to pursue. It looks at you and your teams skills, the market you are going into and the value of what you intend to build. It looks at the risks or challenges you will likely face and how you plan to address them. It might also look at your marketing plan or your product development roadmap.

Ideally these two documents should be created with an external consultant who is experienced in creating business plans and financial forecasts. They should ask the dumb questions and the tough questions that make sense of the business to any rational observer. They might also point out holes in the plan that need to be addressed. It's rarely the case that the same person who is enamoured by the vision of the business is also able to have a stone-cold view of the numbers and the gaps in the plan. It's worth bringing in someone who isn't drunk on the big picture of the business – even if it costs some money, it's typically well worth it.

PRODUCT STRATEGY: THE KEY TO MAKING MONEY FROM YOUR IDEA

From a customer's point of view, your business exists to give them products. A product can be defined as a consistent way of achieving a desired outcome that your customer wants.

When I look at a Rolex, I don't see the product as being a watch. I see the product as 'a conspicuous device that communicates status and high achievement'.

A person who buys a Rolex does not want to buy a device that tells the time. They could buy a $20 Casio that does a better job of telling the time. The desired outcome the customer wants to achieve has more to do with what a Rolex says about the wearer.

If the management at Rolex thought they were in the watch business, they would miss the point of what 'product' they are really selling.

Even a service business exists to deliver an outcome. People go to a massage therapist because they want to feel relaxed, pampered and rejuvenated. If they don't get that outcome it's unlikely they will go back again.

An accountant is there to deliver outcomes like tax compliance, management accounts and business planning. It's true they deliver a service but the customer really sees it as an outcome or a product.

When you think about your product, you need to be very clear about the real problem you are solving. You need to see yourself as someone who is project managing some sort of result for your clients.

If you have a service, you need to structure it in a highly repeatable way so it begins to resemble a product. You should also give your services a special name, like you would a product.

Imagine two accountants. The first one thinks of themself as offering a service: 'tax advice and compliance'. The second one sees themself as a product creator and has three products: 'FinancialFix', 'GrowthPlan' and 'ExitMax'. Which accountant would you rather talk to? Who would earn money and have a business that scales?

The first key to commercialising your business is deciding what product you are actually selling and giving it a name that best reflects the customer need you solve (as an interesting side note, the name 'Rolex' was a made-up word that the founder thought sounded luxurious in any language). This simple decision will largely impact how much money you make for the life of the business.

The next step is choosing how you will take it to market. I am going to recommend that you use a very special product strategy that I have developed, called an 'Ascending Transaction Model' (ATM).

In order to understand why this strategy works I need first to share several strategies that don't work.

Product Strategies that don't Work for Small Business

I've worked with thousands of small business owners over the last 10 years who have come in contact with my training businesses.

What I have noticed is that many of them have a flawed product strategy. From day one, I can tell they will fail simply by the way they are taking their product to market.

Let me share four common product strategies that don't work for small business.

1. ONLY ONE PRODUCT OR SERVICE (OOPS) – TOO BRAND DEPENDENT

This is where a business only has one product or service. You either take it or leave it.

When you ask the owner of an OOPS business what range of products they can sell you, they are likely to say things like: 'I do plumbing, you can buy plumbing services from me.' 'I sell IT services, you can get me to help with your IT problems.'

This is the most common strategy in a traditional small business; and the reason these businesses stay small. It can work if you build a massive brand behind that single product like Zippo lighters or Tabasco sauce did. In most cases, however, a small business rarely ever builds a big enough brand to make an OOPS business work.

2. J Curve – Too Capital Dependent

This is by far the most common and most dangerous business model that people lose money on.

The 'J curve' describes the shape of the cash flow – it loses money before making money. A J-curve business often requires a lot of money to set it up and it has high overheads that have to be covered regardless of how many sales are made.

A typical small example is a restaurant. It costs lots of money to set up a new restaurant. There's the deposit, the leases, the fit out, the equipment, the stock, the marketing, the hiring and training of staff. The restaurant owner has to spend hundreds of thousands of dollars before the doors are even open.

It can take months, or even years, to build up a loyal following of customers who make a restaurant profitable. If you don't have the capital to stay open, you will go broke before you get through the dip.

Even after the doors are open, the running costs aren't small either. Each month a restaurant needs to sell thousands of meals before it covers its costs.

A common feature of a J-curve business is it sells something relatively cheap and you have to sell a lot of them to survive. If you have a slow month, chances are you will lose a lot of money.

Think about an e-commerce business that sells t-shirts for $20. To cover the cost of just one employee would require thousands of sales each year.

Most 'J curve' businesses don't make money for 3–5 years. However, if they make it through the dip, they are very profitable and very valuable – this is the uptick of the J.

A classic example is a successful software company. The software business invests a million dollars developing a digital product that will sell for $50 per month. At first, this business loses money each month but then the sub-scription revenue overtakes the costs and it's all profit from that point on.

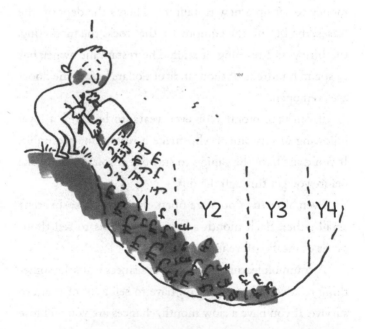

A successful J-curve business is eventually valuable because an acquirer would rather buy something that has made it through the dip rather than go through this risky phase themselves. A J-curve business is an advanced strategy for entrepreneurs who can access capital. It's not a great place to start.

3. One-Stop Shop – Too Systems Dependent

A one-stop shop is a business that tries to sell too many products, or tries to offer too much customisation. Effectively, a customer comes in contact with the business and can make hundreds of product choices.

Amazon is a one-stop shop. Wal-Mart is too. These businesses offer endless product options.

A catering business that lets the customer dictate all of the menu options is creating complexity that is hard to deal with.

The problem with this type of business is there are too many moving parts. Too many things can go wrong. It's too easy for your customers or staff to 'break' the business.

In order to run this sort of business profitably, you need absolutely bulletproof systems. If you don't have the systems in place, you will always be pulling your hair out trying to fight fires.

I often see small businesses that are trying to be all things to everyone. They sell hundreds of products and let customers have limitless ways to customise their order. With all of this choice, it's impossible to get traction with any particular thing. This business is always dealing with some drama that relates to one of its many products or custom orders and it typically fails to build a good brand. Just because you can sell something doesn't mean you should.

4. BROKERAGE MODEL – TOO TIME DEPENDENT

Brokerage businesses sell other people's value. The typical example is a real estate agency or a car yard. They don't own the assets they sell, they go out and put a seller and a buyer together.

My first businesses were brokerage model businesses. I would go and find a product that I thought was going to be hot and I would take it to market.

Despite turning over millions, I was always shocked to discover that these early ventures were not worth real money to investors or acquirers.

Whenever I would get my business valued, I would be told the same thing: 'there's no asset in this business that you own'. One person described my business as a 'sales engine'.

Despite our team, our seven-figure revenue and our offices, if we stopped working the business would grind to an immediate halt.

What I didn't have was intellectual property. It would be cheaper for someone to set up in competition with me than to buy my business. The real value belonged to my clients who owned the business assets.

Despite the downsides of this business model, it is by far the best way to start out in business.

If you've never been in business before, don't go out and invent your own products. Go and find someone who has a successful product and help them to sell more of it or help them to sell it in a new territory.

Two years working as a brokerage for someone else will teach you about business. You won't need to worry about product development, you will just need to get good at sales, marketing and administration – vital skills for any entrepreneur.

If you broker someone else's product, your job is simply to find ways to sell it efficiently. This skill will be invaluable to you later in your business life.

A brokerage business won't really attract investors, it won't sell for much but it will teach you everything you need to know about running a successful business with less risk.

Once you have the basics down, you can then develop your own products in a way that does create real value.

THE ASCENDING TRANSACTION MODEL (ATM)

Products and services don't make profit – product and service ecosystems do. It's the right mix of products and services that creates an elegant product strategy that spits out plenty of money and doesn't have the problems I've highlighted about other strategies.

Let us look at a very powerful product strategy that makes a lot of money. I have called this system an Ascending Transaction Model (ATM) because I want you to remember that it's designed to give you money.

It involves four types of products that strategically work together to generate a lot of revenue. These are the four types of products you must develop:

1. Gifts
2. Products for prospects (PFP)
3. Core offerings
4. Products for clients (PFC)

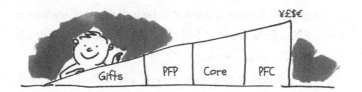

RULES FOR CREATING EACH PRODUCT IN THE ATM

Let's take a look at each of these types of products in order and place some rules around them to make sure they are doing their job.

1. GIFTS

Gifts are free products that you give to the world expecting nothing in return. You don't ask for contact details, you don't ask for money, you don't ask for anything. They are thoughtful, valuable and enticing in their own right and they show just how brilliant your business is.

A great gift is delightful if it's given to the right person at the right time. It needs to open people up to a whole new world of value that your business offers.

Your gift should entice people to want to know more about what you do and what value you offer.

Big companies like Rolex, Qantas, Credit Suisse and Kia give us the tennis, the golf, yacht races and other sporting events as a gift. They pay for these events to run and you don't have to be a customer to enjoy them.

Apple gives you iTunes for free. Google gives you browsers, calendars, maps, apps and more for free.

In a small business, a gift can be a digital masterclass, a book, a YouTube channel full of great content, a downloadable checklist or a sample.

The key is that you give it freely and ask nothing back from the person who receives it.

RULES FOR CREATING A GIFT

1. **It is given as a gift without conditions.** The gift must be given freely, it must be perceived as valuable and timely. You must not ask for anything in return, you release the gift 'free to the world'.

2. **It must be meaningful.** A great gift can open people up to a whole new world; a world where the problems and frustrations they've had don't exist the way they used to.

3. **It doesn't send you broke.** The gift must be low cost for you to deliver; you can't go broke giving gifts. In most cases it will be a digital gift, social media or an event experience (all of these have a very low and manageable cost per person).

2. PRODUCTS FOR PROSPECTS

This is a product for people who want to try you out without committing too much money or time. This type of product is designed to offer a quick win or a first-hand experience. It's a sample of things to come, a test drive or a first step in the right direction.

A software business will have a trial period, a good law firm will offer a free first consultation, a car dealership might invite you to a special event, a small business might get you to buy a home study kit or attend a low-cost seminar.

Products for prospects need to have a low cost – either a small amount of money, some focused time or sharing of contact details.

The product for prospects is designed to ignite the commercial relationship between your business and your ideal customer.

It should warm people up to doing business with you, share some of your philosophy, demonstrate your value and do it all quickly and cheaply.

One of the best examples is the Porsche Experience Center. It offers a thrilling 90-minute track driving experience in a current model car. It's relatively affordable (compared to a car), it's easy to do and it's memorable. Many people start the experience with no intention of buying a Porsche and a short time later they can't stop thinking about it.

My favourite PFPs for small businesses are webinars, memberships, discussion groups, online assessments, quizzes or introduction events.

RULES FOR CREATING A PRODUCT FOR PROSPECTS

1. **Get your ideas out to the world.** The product for prospects should be focused on sharing your ideas and philosophies. Not generic ideas, not old ideas, not small ideas. Share your big, unique and transformational ideas with your prospects. Ideas are cheap these days – make your money on the implementation of the ideas.

2. **Get contact details.** A product for prospects should be exchanged for accurate contact information. It's OK to charge for this product if you like and it's also OK to give it at no charge but you must get people's contact details in the process.

3. **Quick wins that heighten desire.** You want to make sure that people get some sort of quick benefit from this product, preferably in under seven days. If you charge, it should be priced cheaply enough that people feel they got a very good deal, considering how quickly they started to see value. The product for prospects should lead people closer to the decision to buy your core product but not cannibalise your core product. A quick win doesn't mean that the problem is completely solved and there's no longer a need to do more with your business.

3. CORE OFFER

These are the products (or services) you are famous for.

For Porsche, it's cars not experiences. Google's core offering is search, with ads. Singapore Airlines are known for long-haul flights. Deloitte does audit and consulting for big companies.

A business coach might run a workshop as a product for prospects and then offer coaching programmes as a core business. A software company has an online course as a product for prospects and a subscription service as the core offer.

With your core business you deliver a full and remarkable solution to what people want. These products seriously solve problems and you can charge your worth.

They are your main focus and your customers and clients can't stop talking about them. These products are priced to be profitable. It's OK to lose small money on gifts and products for prospects but not on your core business.

You've given people a taste of what you can do with your product for prospects but now it's time to be paid for your fair value when someone wants to access your core business. Your gifts and product for prospects have built up demand for your core offer so you can feel confident that you can charge your worth.

The market won't pay much for salt, but it will pay a lot for 'Himalayan Organic Mineral Rock Salt'. Himalayan salt is special, you can't easily compare it to regular table salt and so it sells for ten times the price of table salt. You need to make sure your customer can understand why your offer is unique in the market.

You must create a special methodology that makes your core offering unique and remarkable. You need to push your team to be the best in your market for this type of product.

It's important that you develop enticing brochures and websites for your core product. You should raise your profile as the leader in your industry for your core product. Win awards and get the top people in your industry endorsing your core offer.

The key is to create a full and remarkable solution to your ideal customer's problem. You want your core product to turn people into evangelists for your brand. Your buyers want products that matter. They want to buy things that have a story. They want things that take them on a journey and that expand their world. They want to intertwine their own story with the products they buy and they want to tell other people.

RULES FOR CREATING A CORE PRODUCT

1. **A remarkable solution.** The core business must be a full and remarkable solution to a real problem your potential clients face. By definition, a remarkable product is something that is worth talking about. Your goal is to create your product in a way that people want to tell their friends how good it is.

   The key to making your product remarkable is to discover how your product or business changes people's lives for the better. Once you know what it is your product does for people, focus heavily on telling those stories through every interaction and make it easy for your customers to tell others about you.

2. **Implementation, not ideas.** In most cases your business will implement some sort of change for a customer or client. You will create something they couldn't create on their own or you will work with them closely to help them create it properly. Do not fall into the trap of thinking that you will make money just by sharing your ideas. We live in a world where people already have access to ideas free of charge; they don't have time to implement the ideas and they want to pay you big money to do it for them (or to get them to do it right). When someone has your core product they feel it solved a problem or created a huge benefit.

3. **The price is right.** The job of the core product is to make profit; you can break even or even lose small money on gifts and products for prospects but you must never undersell your core product at a loss or a break even.

Your core product can't be the same as everything else in the market. A commodity sells for the lowest price; you can't afford to let your product or service be seen as just another version of the same thing. Commodities are easy to compare, de-commoditised products aren't.

To avoid a J-curve, the core offer should not be low cost, high-volume sale. Unless your business has funding, a core offer is usually something that generates over $1000 revenue per customer per year.

4. PRODUCTS FOR CLIENTS

Your core product was so delightful that your clients want to know what comes next. The PFC products are the products you mostly sell to people who've already bought your core business.

Porsche are known for their cars but they make a lot of money in finance and insurance (the logical next step after you've just bought a car). Then they service your vehicle and eventually they handle the sale of your older car as they upgrade you to their new model.

A business coach might gift books, then run a workshop as a PFP and then offer coaching packages as the core offer. This coach might then create a special annual retreat for clients to attend. This three-day annual retreat could attract enough clients at a high price to significantly add to the annual profit.

Your PFC should be highly profitable. The cost of winning the relationship has already been covered so PFCs have an extra layer of profit margin built in.

The best PFCs are subscription products like memberships, software, insurance, support services. These recurring revenue streams take time to build but once they start stacking up they are the long-term underpinning of your business.

With this fourth product in your ecosystem you should do well in business for many years to come.

RULES FOR CREATING A PRODUCT FOR CLIENTS

1. **It's highly profitable.** The PFC should aim to double the profitability of your business. This product is designed to be sold to existing clients so you don't have the huge costs of building a relationship with them. A well-selected second product should have the potential to double the profit in your business.

2. **It's different.** It must not simply be more of the same. If your core business is accounting, your PFC can't be more accounting in some other form; instead it could be legal services, business coaching, software, temping staff, software and so on. Something other than your core offer repackaged.

3. **It's logical.** You don't want to confuse your clients with a second product offering that just doesn't fit with your brand. If you sell graphic design services, you don't want to offer fitness training as a second sale because it just doesn't make sense. The PFC is a 'logical next step' that

shows up after you solved the first problem. For example, after a fitness trainer helps their client lose weight the client logically wants to buy new clothes; the fitness trainer could add a personal image consulting service to their business.

These Products Fit Together in a Product Ecosystem

These four types of product are designed to string together and create a product ecosystem. They take a client on a journey from barely knowing your business to feeling great about doing a lot of business with you.

Your potential clients will appreciate a gift that is given in the spirit of being thoughtful.

They will then want to try out something without too much risk. They might be happy to spend a small amount of money for a quick win. Your product for prospects is the perfect thing for them to try you out.

After having two positive experiences with your business, a client may now be open to spending money on your core business. You can also bet they are the right kind of client because they now have a better understanding of you too.

If your core business is as good as you've said it is, your client will have other wants, needs or problems that they would like you to help them with. Your PFC product will be the perfect thing.

As I said, most of the costs in acquiring a client have already been absorbed in the previous products so you may discover that you end up earning more profit on the PFC than in your core.

If you do it correctly, you will have constructed a seamless journey for your clients. They will enjoy dealing with you because they don't feel pressured or rushed to make a big decision; they feel each decision is quite natural and is based on positive past experiences with you and your business.

CREATING THE ECOSYSTEM THAT LINKS YOUR PRODUCTS

It's not enough simply to have these four types of products in your business. You need the glue that links them up to form an ecosystem.

There are three key pieces of 'glue' that hold your ATM together.

1. LEAD CAPTURE PROCESS

You need to capture people's details. Prospective clients need to be able to signal to you that they are interested in doing business by registering their contact details with you.

This first piece of glue sits between your gift and your PFP. A lot of people who receive your gift product will want to engage with you. Make sure they can easily find a way to register for the next thing.

This could be on your website (e.g. fill in your details and then download our research paper). It could be a good old-fashioned fishbowl on the counter for people to put their business card in. It could be an online quiz that people complete. It could be that you train your staff how to ask for key information when they interact with potential customers. It could be a Facebook group that requires people to give their contact information to join. However you structure it, cap-turing people's contact details is a key part of your business and you should have several ways to collect them.

Start to become more aware of how other companies capture your details. You might be surprised to discover that you are handing over your details several times per week in various forms. Additionally, research the people in your industry and find out who is capturing details in a profes-sional and brand-affirming way. Take these lead-capturing processes and put them into your business.

2. SALES CONVERSATIONS

The next piece of glue is sales. It's a very important part of every business that many small business owners often avoid.

Secretly, many small business owners have a negative association to selling and they wish they could simply do extra marketing, extra servicing or extra networking rather than having to have the sales conversation.

Unfortunately, this is a fantasy. LVMH, Ferrari, Google, HSBC and Apple all invest in sales training so their staff know how to have a structured sales conversation with a prospective buyer.

If the world's biggest brands, with the world's hottest products, need to have sales conversations then so does every small business.

The good news is, if someone has had a good experi-ence with your gift and products for prospects, the sales conversation will be an enjoyable experience. Products for prospects and gifts are brilliant for warming people up to be pre-sold before they meet you for a sales chat.

In many cases, a person who has experienced your product for prospects already suspects they want to do business with you but they just need to clarify some finer points and sort out the particulars.

I would go so far as to say that you or your sales people should avoid talking to people unless they have experienced a product for prospects. If someone calls out of the blue and wants to talk business, be sure to send them the gift or the product for prospects before you meet with them.

I recommend that you become more keenly interested in how sales conversations are structured. Go and put yourself in situations where you can be sold to, find out what works for you as a buyer and what doesn't. See if you can create the ultimate 'buying experience' out of your sales conversations.

3. Servicing Process

The final piece of glue is servicing your clients after they buy your core offer. Your clients need you to look after them better than you said you would.

You must strategically undersell your core product. You must keep some aces up your sleeve and resist the temptation to tell prospects about everything you will do for them once they are a client.

If you offer 24-hour support, don't mention it unless you absolutely have to – let it be a surprise. If you send out a special box of goodies to your clients, try to keep this quiet so it feels amazing when it arrives.

If you tell your clients everything you do it will stop being special, they will expect it. When the invite arrives for the special river cruise you don't want them to think 'they did what they said they were going to do'. You want people buzzing that you went above and beyond.

Even after you've delivered value to your clients, they will want to know that they are still valued and you're still available to them. You must build into your business special ways to look after your existing clients, long after they have bought from you.

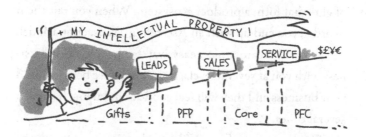

You can put them into an online club membership or forum, you can invite them to 'clients only' events, you can send them updates. Make sure it's delightful though.

If you send out a half-hearted newsletter once a month it will have the opposite effect on your clients: rather than being delighted by you, they will be annoyed.

If people are delighted by your servicing, they will want to buy your PFC. If you fail to service your existing clients, no matter how good your core product is, it's unlikely you will get an uptake on your next offering.

Think of all the businesses you have bought from in the last year or two. See if you can think of who has looked after you as a client above and beyond your expectations.

Can you recall special events, little surprises or unexpected value that showed up after you were already a client? If not, can you imagine what you would have loved them to do? When you have some ideas, design some surprises for your existing clients.

THE COMPLETE ATM

Now you have the four products and you have three pieces of glue that form a product ecosystem. When you put them in order, you end up with an Ascending Transaction Model.

You will create a nice, easy way for people to do business with you at several levels. People will love being around your business and they will feel good about buying from you several times.

The best part of an ATM is that you can simply go around making sure people get given gifts and products for prospects. After that, the domino effect kicks in and you have a business that just flows.

WHAT HAPPENS WHEN YOU DON'T HAVE A PRODUCT ECOSYSTEM?

It takes time to create an ATM. You put many hours into strategy, design and production in order to get it right.

Failing to do so, however, shouldn't be an option.

Many small business people want their business to be easy and simple so they just don't bother to put together an ATM.

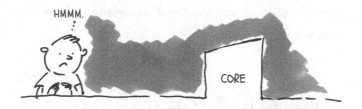

With too few products, they make the error of pushing their core business too soon. They expect people who hardly know them to open their wallet and start spending.

When this doesn't happen, the business owner makes the mistake of lowering the price of the core business to a level that isn't profitable and they begin to resent their business and their clients.

If they don't lower the price, too few potential customers make the leap. They might be charging a fair price but simply don't have enough clients to run the business.

The issue isn't the price of the core product; the issue is that the business has not created a relationship; something the gift and product for prospects are designed to do.

Even if the business has these first three products it will be profitable. However, without the PFC, the business is probably doing barely half the profit it is capable of.

An Ascending Transaction Model covers your bases. It has products that build relationships and products that deliver value. It gets you out to market and it makes you money.

The key is taking time to carefully plan and produce the products you will have in your ATM. If you simply give up,

you're destined to stay small and struggle to make money
from your venture.

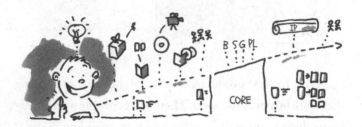

A Big Lesson or Big Result

Not only have I used the ATM strategy to grow several
multimillion dollar businesses myself, I've used this formula with hundreds of my clients and it's staggering how
fast their businesses become dramatically more profitable.

I've seen a personal trainer go from £50k a year to £200k
a year in one year. I've seen a consultant go from £80k a year
to £500k in just 20 months after implementing an ATM.
I've seen a charity go from $2.5m a year in donations to $4m
the following year using this strategy.

I've seen it work with all sorts of businesses and charities.

When you put the ATM into your business one of two
things will happen very quickly:

1. Either you will get a big result and start seeing your business succeed.
2. Or you will discover that your business idea is lacking
   something very fundamental and you need to make a
   big change.

Unfortunately, until you have an elegant business model like the Ascending Transaction Model, you simply won't know.

It's easy to blame the economy, the competition, the government, the clients or the staff. If your business is underperforming, I urge you not to blame any external factor until after you've implemented an ATM strategy with excellence. After that, you can go looking for another reason.

Maybe your idea is great or maybe it sucks; it's impossible to tell unless you've tested out how that product fits with your ATM.

A single product out on its own won't tell you much. It might be an amazing core offering but, without a product for prospects helping it along, it might not sell.

You might have a created a great product for prospects, but you just don't have a remarkable core offering to back it up.

It's important to know the ATM isn't an overnight phenomenon. It's a powerful strategy but it can take time to implement.

You need to create products that you are proud of. My clients often take between 6 and 12 months to get their ATM just right. Many discover on day one that they don't have a core offering and they have been trying to rest their business upon a product for prospects.

This is a good framework but it's not valuable until it becomes more than just an idea.

In the next part of this book, I'm going to focus on overcoming the roadblocks to implementation. I want to discuss what's required for you to go from a good idea to an exceptional business.

In the chapter ahead, you'll discover what you must focus on in order to be successful as an entrepreneur and make the most of the times we are living in.

CHAPTER 6

YOUR CORE TEAM

BUILD YOUR TEAM

Everything great is created by a team. They say it takes a village to raise a child. Building a successful business is certainly not something you do on your own either.

Even when you see a champion tennis player alone on the court, you know he got there as a result of the people around him as well as his talent. It took a coach, a manager, a physiotherapist, a dietician and an assistant to make it possible for one person to play at that elite level.

Successful entrepreneurship relies upon a team getting into alignment. The entrepreneur builds the team and the team builds the business. An entrepreneur's job is to be the organising force, not to actually do the work. Great entrepreneurs like Richard Branson, Steve Jobs and Elon Musk are not highly qualified technically. They are talented enough to spot talent, they bring together great people and point them in the direction of success. A great entrepreneur rarely does the thing, they get the thing done.

Team Building Lessons from the British Military

The British Army has been functioning for about 400 years and has probably experimented with every team-building activity and structure ever conceived.

Scout Team – this is a team of two people whose job is to explore and gather information. In business, any time you have an idea for a new product, innovation or market, assign a two-person scout team to explore it. The scout team should consist of one person whose main focus is sales and marketing and the other person whose main focus is operational excellence. One person is going to test to see if the idea is a good fit with what customers want and the second person will look into the reality of delivering it to them.

This pair (often co-founders) are perfectly adequate for creating and testing a minimum viable product (MVP). This MVP could take the form of a basic website with the ability to join a waiting-list, an introduction event for a small group of potential clients, an online group or an assessment. Proving or disproving assumptions is really the only goal for this team – they are a pair of scientists conducting experiments and gathering data.

For example, you might decide that you want to create a new software product. You assign a scout team to this project to spend a month or two looking into the viability of this new project. One person will talk to potential customers, find out what their problems are, how much they'd be willing to spend for a solution and who the competitors are. The other person will talk to the developers and designers to see how much it will cost to build the software, how many people will be needed to run it and provide customer service. The two people will be in constant contact while they are exploring and will then report back with what they find. In your first venture, it's likely that you will be one of these people.

Fire Team – this is a four-person team designed to do something fast and high impact like a sales campaign, launch event or an urgent product upgrade. In the military, this team is used when there's only one urgent outcome required and the stakes are high. I like using a small four-person team to launch something new and get the first 100–1000 customers engaged. This little team is perfect for executing a special launch event, raising money or running a pilot programme with clients. The four people will typically have one senior person who's leading the team, a sales person, an operations person and an assistant or admin person.

These four go-getters are looking for something called product–market fit (PMF). They are trying to find something a group of people will willingly purchase and be happy with. They need to make fast iterations or pivots to mould their product to the shape of the market's desire. Like blacksmiths bashing away at steel, they remove imperfections and forge something that stands a chance at scaling up.

For example, you've decided to go ahead with the software business and you need to raise money from investors. You assign a four-person fire team to put together an investor presentation for 30–40 angel investors. The team builds a list of suitable angels, contacts them and invites them to a Zoom meeting where they are presented with the plan. The team collects expressions of interest and then has individual conversations with investors to secure the funding round.

Section – this is typically eight people who form a team that will work together day in and day out to achieve a variety of goals. This team normally has two more senior people who lead the other six towards successful outcomes. One of the senior people should be market facing and focused on the big picture – speaking to clients, going on podcasts, giving talks, winning deals and being the voice of the team. The other senior person should be very task focused – managing the team, measuring results, correcting errors, getting the practical day-to-day work done with the team. The team should have a mix of sales and marketing, technical or operations and finance or administration people.

Thos core team is responsible for preparing a go-to-market (GTM) approach. Now armed with a product people want, they are more concerned with finding channels to sell through and platforms for growth. They are looking for clues on how the product will achieve scale and on creating assets the business will use to drive growth.

For example, you got the funding and now you are launching the software business. You have a lead developer who will work with a designer and software engineer to build the software. You also have the charismatic founder who is going to run around signing up clients and will generate enterprise leads for the sales person to follow up on. You also have a financial controller and marketing executive who are managing cashflow and creating advertising campaigns.

Platoon – a platoon is typically a team of 30–50 people with multiple sub-teams being led by a leadership team. The leadership team is typically 3–6 people who each have 4–8 people on their sub-teams. The goal of a platoon is to become an established and dominant force in their territory or market.

This dynamic team of teams are focused on executing the GTM strategy. They are opening up channels to market and selling. They are kicking the doors off the hinges and making sure the business achieves sufficient growth to be valuable. They are also keeping an eye out for the next big move that will lead to scaling up again and again. They might be assigning a scout team to explore a new territory to enter, a new product innovation or a new market of buyers they hadn't yet connected with.

For example, the software business has grown successfully and found a niche serving small wealth management firms in London, New York and Singapore. The business has a leadership team of five people. The chief operations officer (COO) has a service and delivery team, HR and admin. The chief financial officer (CFO) has a financial controller and bookkeeper. The chief executive officer (CEO) is out talking to customers and speaks at the industry conferences, troubleshooting hard problems and making sure the company is aligned to the most important objectives.

In the military, the next size team is a company, which is typically 150+ people and then there's a battalion and a regiment that incorporates thousands of people. The most entrepreneurial teams are the smaller ones from 2 to 50 people. After that, you are starting to become a more grown-up organisation that requires leadership, governance and more advanced funding options – topics to explore at a later date.

CREATE A HIGH PERFORMANCE CULTURE FROM THE START

If you have the ingredients discussed in the previous chapter, you are ready to *begin* your journey and advance through the seven phases of the Entrepreneur Revolution.

Along the way you will encounter many difficult choices. Every entrepreneur's journey is complex and, without the right culture, you simply can't make the right decisions consistently.

The best way to cultivate this culture is through 'maxims'. In business, maxims are designed to be principles of high performance.

Maxims represent a core philosophy designed to inspire a way of being that produces the results you want.

Maxims are your compass. They are home truths, or principles, that help guide you through the complexity of building your empire from concept to multinational operation.

Facebook has maxims like 'move fast and break things' and 'fail faster' to maintain its risk-taking, start-up culture.

Nike has maxims like 'We're on the offensive always' and 'It's in our nature to innovate' to keep them on track as a competitive sporting brand.

I am going to share with you the maxims of high performance that have helped guide me through the seven layers. These maxims have helped me to perform – despite recessions, setbacks and costly mistakes.

Attempt to adopt them as your own. When you are ready, I also encourage you to develop your own maxims that inspire you even more.

MAXIM 1: YOU GET WHAT YOU PITCH FOR ... AND YOU ARE ALWAYS PITCHING

A pitch is a powerful set of words that you deliver to the world again and again. Eventually, if you stick at it and really get the pitch perfected, you will get what you pitch for.

In your business, if you get your pitch right you can raise money, attract a team, engage partners and inspire new clients. If you are a change maker with a great pitch, you will eventually attract a following, upset the status quo and see a shift in your cause.

A client of mine, Toby Milden, was told by his school that because of his disability, he would be able to get a job peeling boiled eggs if he was lucky. Toby wasn't having it and he pitched his local bank manager and got a job at a major bank. He then pitched his way into the senior roles at the BBC, Accenture and Deloitte. Today he has a successful business consulting to FTSE100 companies on how to bring in a more diverse talent pool, he's an author and speaks at conferences across the country. His pitching skills have resulted in countless people being able to work in big business brands across the UK.

Another example is my friend, Jeremy Gilley. In 1999 he began to pitch 'I believe the world needs a day of peace which will serve humanity as a starting point for bringing us together despite our differences.' By 2001, Jeremy found himself in the United Nations witnessing a unanimous resolution for a fixed calendar day of peace (21 September). He got what he pitched for; today over 100 million people celebrate Peace Day each year.

A powerful pitch, delivered hundreds of times, will allow you to speak your best ideas into reality; but it doesn't end there.

When you repetitively pitch a bad idea that doesn't help you it will have just as much power. If you are consistently pitching people 'I have no money because, as a child, my parents complained about not having enough' you will also speak it into reality. People will begin to reinforce your belief, support you in making it real, and reinforce its validity. You will get what you pitch for and you will have no money!

Pitch 'the economy is so bad now' and it will start to materialise as people with money to spend think twice about sending it your way. Pitch 'it's impossible to find good employees' and the amazing people you wish to hire will get a sense this isn't the right place to work.

Choose your words carefully – at some level, everything you say out loud is a pitch.

Entrepreneurship is the journey of a thousand pitches. To be successful, you are going to be pitching your business over and over again for years.

You get to choose what you want to pitch for. If you choose to pitch yourself and your business as small, insignificant and pedestrian, don't be surprised when you get that result. Your business will never outperform the way you pitch it.

Pitching is powerful, so be deliberate with your words because you will get what you pitch for and you are always pitching. Train your team how to deliver a powerful pitch every time someone asks them 'what do you do?'

Maxim 2: Influence Comes from Output ... Not Confidence

Don't wait until you feel confident in your abilities before you create something. Confidence is not required.

Take a look at Whitney Houston, Kurt Cobain, John Candy and Amy Winehouse, and you won't see people who were supremely self-confident. You will see people who were perpetually tormented by their insecurities, plagued by self-doubt and a lack of confidence resulting in their own demise. Yet they were all massively influential.

Influence is not about confidence, influence is about output. You can lack confidence, you can be racked by self-doubt and you can secretly fear an imminent alien invasion *but* if you create amazing output you will gather influence.

Influencers are producers. We only know about influential people because of their prolific output.

They might have big houses and fancy things but that's not how they became influential. They create, not consume, for their influence.

The Beatles created the world's most valuable music catalogue in just eight years; they were prolific, not confident.

Stephen Spielberg has written over 20 screenplays, directed over 50 films and produced close to 200 movies; he's prolific, not confident.

Oprah Winfrey did 4561 episodes of her iconic talk show, she's written five books, published monthly magazines and produced daily radio shows; she's prolific, not confident.

Steve Jobs built three separate companies, was listed as the inventor on 317 patents, and is credited as reinventing seven industries; he was prolific, not confident.

It is creation that creates influence. It's your ability to write and publish, record and duplicate, design and produce. It's your ability to finish the job and put a completed product into the world.

The idea that influencers are simply cool, hip or trendy is superficial. It overlooks the enormous amounts of energy that influencers put into constantly producing and publishing output.

It does not matter if you are confident or not. Produce something of value, create a product, publish a book, make a video, prototype a widget. Eventually you will create something excellent and it will give you more influence.

I've worked with dozens of people on creating new things. Most of the people I've worked with had self-doubts to begin with, but we pushed to keep producing. Often the confidence came after the project was complete, but not before.

Logically, real confidence can only come *after* you have done something. It may never come at all. Fear not, it doesn't matter, keep creating and your influence will go through the roof.

Don't let your perfectionism stand in the way either; prolific beats perfect too. Getting stuff done will create more momentum than waiting for everything to be perfect.

Creating all the time is fun and it generates all sorts of results. Wealth, influence, recognition and joy all flow from creating. Make sure your team is not afraid to put their work into the world.

MAXIM 3: INCOME FOLLOWS ASSETS

Your job each year is to create new assets. An asset is anything that would still be valuable if you were hit by a bus.

Using this definition, it's easy to see why a house or shares are assets. If you were hit by a bus, your house and your shares wouldn't change in value.

In business it's exactly the same. Your business needs to be built so that it would still be valuable if you disappeared.

To do this, you need intellectual property, media and technology assets that are unique to your business. You must develop systems, methods and procedures. You need a brand and a culture. You need a system of marketing and selling your products and services.

When your business is in a position to carry on without you, then you have built yourself a whopping big asset.

You don't need to be overwhelmed by this concept. It takes time to build a whole business that can continue on without you. However, you can chip away at it each year.

Create documents. Every year create more and more of them. Sales scripts, training manuals, brochures, reports, checklists and best practices.

Put them in writing, get a graphic designer to make them look pretty, then make sure they get used. It seems challenging at first. However, pretty soon, you can't imagine running a business without them.

My business coach gave me some harsh advice when I was really struggling. I had been through a tough year and had considered selling my business for just £300k. He looked at my business and said 'Income follows assets but you haven't built many.'

Under my nose we discovered several great ideas that hadn't been documented. For a year, our team became driven to create documents, media assets, posters and workbooks and 12 months later the business was valued at £4m!

Your business will take off when you start putting your time into asset creation rather than just doing the work. Be sure to train your team on how to identify opportunities for asset creation.

ACTIVITY: Visit www.24assets.com to discover what assets you already have in your business and to identify opportunities to develop more.

MAXIM 4: GET KNOWN BY THE SUCCESS OF YOUR CLIENTS

The best way to become famous is for what you have done for others.

If you focus on creating success for your clients, they will go out and tell the world. People are unlikely to believe what you say about yourself, but they will be very impressed by the favourable stories your clients are telling about you.

Most great businesses grow because of what others are saying about them. Google grew because people showed others how magical the results are when you 'Google' something. Facebook grew because of the sentence 'are you on Facebook?' spoken between friends. Apple's meteoric growth in the 2000s was down to 'raving Apple fans'.

My own business success really took off when we focused centrally on the success of our clients as our business and marketing strategy.

As soon as people started hearing our client success stories, we had people beating down the door.

When it came time to invest in a social media campaign, we sent camera crews out to our clients' offices and let our clients tell their stories. As a result, we have dozens of video case studies that help us to generate all the business we can handle.

Rather than you beating the drum for yourself, beat the drum for your clients. Help them create a huge success story and then showcase it.

In many industries, if you genuinely do focus on the success of your clients, you will stand out like a beacon.

You must ensure your team knows that your business measures its success based on the results your clients get. When they spot the right opportunity, it's essential they find a way to capture the story and share it far and wide.

MAXIM 5: YOU ARE IN PARTNERSHIP WITH EVERYONE WHO TOUCHES YOUR BUSINESS

Seeing everyone who touches your business as a partner is a radical shift away from short-term, transactional behaviour towards long-term success for everyone.

See your team as partners, your suppliers as partners and even your customers as partners. Take the extra time to explore what success really looks like for everyone involved. Create deeper alignment in the needs and wants of everyone who's interacting with your business.

Don't see your business as an independent entity that can survive all on its own. See your business for what it is: a set of relationships that must last if success is to be achieved.

I'm not saying that you can never fire a poor-performing staff member or you can't end a supply deal on a product that isn't working out. Of course, any relationship can grow and evolve and it can also part ways when there's no longer alignment.

Transactional relationships are geared around getting the most out of an exchange in the immediate short term. The spirit of a good partnership is about working together to create success, now and in the future, for everyone involved.

Sometimes this means you can't take an immediate win in the short term and you have to look at the bigger picture.

When the pandemic hit, many big, cashed-up companies saw it as an opportunity to squeeze their suppliers and extend payment terms so they didn't have to pay suppliers for months after the invoice. In the short term they would definitely get a win by squeezing their suppliers for every drop but, in the long term, these suppliers begin to go bust, they look for ways to cut corners, they get sloppy and they simply can't produce their best work.

In some rare cases, big companies like the British retailer Waitrose worked closely with their suppliers to ensure they could ride out the recession and still produce good products. They found ways to support their long-term suppliers who were vulnerable; as a result, their suppliers found ways to help Waitrose. Their premium price brand has expanded over the decades despite recessions and pandemics.

The spirit of partnership is a powerful driving force. It makes us think about the needs of others and work towards creating long-term success for everyone involved. Get your team to focus on win-win partnerships rather than quick-win deals and you will build a business that is solid and reliable for years to come.

MAXIM 6: IDEAS ARE WORTHLESS, IMPLEMENTATION IS EVERYTHING

One of the most frustrating experiences of being well connected in the world of business is the constant question: 'What do you think of my idea?'

My response normally shocks people. I say: 'Ideas are worthless.'

Anyone can sit around and have a big idea. Few can make it brilliant.

Let me give you two examples to illustrate my point.

Most Londoners love the experience of grabbing a sandwich from the UK fast-food sandwich giant, Pret A Manger. Pret stores are clean, the food is good, the service is friendly and you rarely have to wait too long in line. For that reason there are hundreds of Pret stores and the business is worth tens of millions of pounds.

Can you imagine the founders asking the question: 'We're going to make sandwiches; what do you think of our amazing idea?'

It's a dull idea. No one is going to get excited about a sandwich shop. Not until it's implemented with excellence. Even a boring idea becomes valuable when implemented insanely well.

In 2002, Bill Gates was telling people that the tablet PC would be the future of personal computing, so why isn't Microsoft the company famous for introducing us to these devices? They had the idea for tablet PCs in 2002; Steve Jobs didn't release the iPad until 2010!

Microsoft didn't implement the idea beyond its prototype. They waited around to watch Apple conduct the world's most successful product launch. Apple implemented the launch of this product so perfectly that they control the market for tablet PCs, and no one seems to be able to catch them.

In the example of Pret, a boring idea, beautifully implemented, became a hugely successful business. In the case of Microsoft's tablet PC, a brilliant idea, poorly executed, created no real value at all.

The value is in implementation. It's one thing to know that an Ascending Transaction Model would be good for your business, but it's a dedication to excellent implementation that will produce the results.

Having an idea is easy. Creating something is difficult. Creating something takes focus, discipline and dedication.

The word 'creative' used to refer to the power to get something done. In some circles, however, it's come to mean 'possessing the power to think things up'.

Regularly, I hear people say to me: 'My problem is I never finish things because I'm too creative'.

I've also had people say to me: 'I'm not very creative, but I'm very good at getting things done'.

This tells me we have lost our way when it comes to understanding what it means to be 'creative'.

We've bought into the myth that what's going on in someone's head has value in the real world; it doesn't.

Thinking about murdering someone doesn't make you a murderer. Thinking about having a date with Jenifer Lawrence doesn't make you her new boyfriend.

Thinking about a business idea, a product or a new service doesn't make you its 'creator'.

What makes you creative is your ability to bring it into the world in a way that other people can understand and value.

As long as it's in your head, you haven't created anything yet. You must get it out into the real world in a way that shows up as valuable.

We need to use the word 'imaginative' for people who have a lot of ideas. Imaginative people love to dream things up but the word does not imply they have brought their ideas into the world.

Being creative isn't easy; you need to decide upon the idea and then do everything required to bring it into the world. The process can take months or years to get a single creation completed. It's blood, sweat, tears, risk and sacrifice.

We should separate the dreamers from the doers and give more credit to the people who are truly creating things into existence.

MAXIM 7: RESOURCES GO TO THE RESOURCEFUL

It's easy to make excuses that something can't be done because you don't have the resources. Every great entrepreneur started out with far less resources than they needed. They didn't have the money, the team, the distribution channels, the trusted brand or the technology they needed to succeed but they found a way to get those things.

Being resourceful requires you to keep coming back to the fact that we live in a time where there's more money on the planet, more talented people on the planet and more access to great ideas than ever before in history. These resources already exist; you need only to go get them.

No amount of emotional frustration will help you get these resources; you don't get what you throw a tantrum for, you get what you *pitch* for.

If every time you get asked 'how are you?' you respond by saying 'there's no money, there's no time, there are no good people' you will 'pitch it into existence.'

The person listening will not respond by saying 'let me solve all your problems for you.' They will politely agree with you and reaffirm your view. Even if they have time, money or talent they will withhold it from you because they sense there could be good reasons why others aren't giving you resources.

Imagine if you respond to the question with: 'I have so many good opportunities right now. I have opportunities for talented people to join my team. I also have opportunities where extra capital can be used to create valuable assets in my business.' That pitch will get more people interested in helping you and investing in you.

If you want something new, you have to go get it. Resourcefulness is all about having resourceful conversations that move you in the right direction. It's about asking for the things you want until you get them.

It's about dwelling on possible solutions rather than the dead ends. Very few people care about your complaints; they are too busy doing their own thing. Most successful people believe that if you live in a developed economy you don't have much to complain about, you just need to get on with it.

Once you're in a resourceful state and you are having resourceful conversations, it's just a matter of sticking to the path. After you know what needs doing, you must be willing to be held accountable for getting the results.

How do you get into a resourceful state? You must commit. It's only when you are committed that you will become resourceful, not beforehand. When you have put your name on something, you figure it out. Rarely do you get past the discomfort if you have an easy way to back out.

Many teams will say, if you first give us the resources we will create something great. It doesn't work like that. You need your team to commit to creating something great and then go get the resources.

> To see Daniel talk about these maxims for high performance visit: www.dent.global/talk-maxims

THE VALUE CREATION CYCLE

You now have seven maxims that create a culture of high performance but what is it your team will do to grow the business?

There's a predictable cycle that turns ideas into remarkably valuable creations.

You start out as imaginative, coming up with ideas that could work and you end up creating valuable products and businesses that make supernormal profits.

The journey along the way is entirely predictable:

1. **Ideas.** Your team needs to surface ideas to take to market. You should have regular sessions with your team to make lists of ideas that would improve your customers' lives. Focus your attention on ideas that directly impact

your customer or allow you to deliver the same value more efficiently. Make lists of problems and then come up with ideas for solving them. Come up with ideas for new product or new markets to enter. Play brainstorming games like 'What would Elon Musk do if he owned this business?' Rank your ideas based on their impact and the cost to implement them.

2. **Testing.** Implementing ideas is always more expensive and time consuming than you first expect. It's also unlikely that your ideas deliver as much value as you first believed. For this reason you must create quick and cheap tests for your ideas before you run full-throttle into developing them fully. I like to run a survey or a quiz that gives me more data. I often run an introduction event so I can present an idea to clients and see how they respond. For a big idea I will get a brochure designed with mock-up illustrations to see how people respond. My favourite strategy is to open up a waiting list for the new idea to see how many people join.

3. **The Beta Version.** Your first step towards launching something new is to create a beta version. You should do this as quickly and cheaply as possible too, so if the feedback is bad you can make changes without much fuss. A beta product could actually be a competitor's product that you white label or alter for the purposes of illustrating your points of difference. The key here is to create something that people can interact with – they touch, feel, listen or experience it and then give you genuine

insights based on a shared reality of your idea. Your goal is to achieve something called 'product–market fit' where you know with certainty that what you will create is going to add value to customers.

4. **The Commercial Version.** When you take on board the feedback from customers and you are sure your business is doing something that matters, it's time to figure out how you will roll this out to more people. At this point you might need to solve problems of scale. You'll need to develop the product and the channels to market. You will probably need to build digital assets and maybe even develop technology and media. The commercial version is ready to go out and sell day to day. People will consider it against other commercial products or services and some people will then pay a normal price for your version. A commercial version must generate enough money to cover your time in selling and producing it. It will often feel disappointing that it's harder to get traction than you first thought. I regularly see people spend a year starting up a business get discouraged when they aren't making an equivalent of their previous wage. Originally, they had imagined their product, service or business was going to make a lot of money or provide a lot of freedom. Now it turns out that all the blood, sweat and tears barely pays a wage – and it requires more work too! At this point, many people believe their idea is flawed and so they go back to the drawing board and have a completely new set of ideas. This begins the cycle again. People who 'make it'

push through to the next step and build something that stands out as valuable.

5. **The remarkable and scalable version.** A remarkable product, service or business is one that people start to tell their friends about. It does something different – it's fresh, it's unique and it's valuable. Because people are talking about it, you get inbound enquiries, you make easier sales, you seem to be in demand and often you can charge a higher price. When you had a commercial version, it felt as if it was all about trading your time for money and it was competitive. When you push past the ordinary you create something special! It's not enough to be impressive, you also need to discover how you can be impressive at scale. The energy required to take a commercial version to a remarkable and scalable version is considerably more than all the energy that went into creating a commercial version. The commercial version got you into the market, but the remarkable and scalable version is what everyone in the market wants to create. In order to build something remarkable and scalable, you have to lean into the innovation process. You have to be willing to improve every detail. A remarkable and scalable business has a remarkable website, a remarkable sales process that scales, a remarkable service process that scales, remarkable designs, a scalable way of attracting remarkable team members, and the list goes on. Your team must become obsessed with the difficult task of making everything more remarkable and scalable.

A great entrepreneur sets the direction and then brings in the team to build out their vision. Becoming a remarkable and scalable business isn't easy but it's worth it. It is a journey that requires creativity, energy, focus and discipline but the results can be sensational. Your team will have fun, bond together, feel a deep sense of pride and share in the rewards that come from success.

THE JOURNEY INTO THE ENTREPRENEUR REVOLUTION

There is a predictable journey you are going to go on as you leave the industrial age and enter the Entrepreneur Revolution.

Without knowing this predictable journey you may get frustrated at times. Maybe things seem like they aren't moving fast enough, or maybe too fast. Maybe you try to run before you can crawl and end up falling down again and again. Maybe you find yourself on a plateau without a clear path to go to the next level.

Without a clear journey you won't make the best of these times you are living in. For that reason, I've mapped out what I consider to be the predictable path you are likely to take as you fully embrace the Entrepreneur Revolution.

The first part of the journey is 'work'. It feels like work and it's where most of us get started.

Work wasn't designed to make you wealthy or fulfilled. It was designed to make you enough money and grant you enough satisfaction that you don't cause a problem for your employer or for society. Work is the comfy little treadmill that you are expected to run on to keep the industrialised society functioning.

Today, the purpose of work is to discover what you love, to get experience and to meet other people in your field. It still isn't designed to make you wealthy but it's there to lay the foundations.

THE THREE LEVELS OF 'WORK'

LEVEL 1: THE NEWBIE

The newbie is fresh, new and enthusiastic in a particular vocation or role. Their job is to learn the ropes and become functional. Often a newbie is called an apprentice. Everyone must do their time as an apprentice. If you are lucky, you will do an apprenticeship under a great mentor and you will set yourself up for a fast-track tour of the workforce. Most people, however, will simply do their training, become functional and then progress to the next level.

LEVEL 2: THE WORKER

After sufficient time in an apprentice role, you become functional and ready to be a worker. You can now do the things you were trained to do by your mentor and you can perform the tasks that will create value for someone who's organising your labour. You might become ambitious in the workforce and seek out a new mentor who will help prepare you for higher levels of functionality.

You may even find yourself working your way up the job ladder and doing very important work. Most people in society never go beyond this level; they bounce between apprentice and worker their whole career, always staying in the comfort zone where they don't want to rock the boat. A small group of people have an entrepreneurial seizure and decide they should work for themselves at the next level.

LEVEL 3: SELF-EMPLOYED

Self-employment might seem like a big, exciting change for a worker. However, little do they realise that they lack some crucial ingredients as an entrepreneur. As a worker, they were trained to believe that value is all about functionality.

The more functional you are the more valuable you are.

Subconsciously, they take these beliefs into their own enterprise and create even more work for themselves. As a worker, they had regular pay, support and didn't need to worry how the whole organisation performed. Now they have their old job to do plus a ton of other jobs that they never really considered until after they were self-employed. They find themselves having to make sales, compile accounts, fix IT problems, manage workflow, come up with strategies and even make the coffee too.

The first three levels make up the vast bulk of society currently. Only a tiny fraction of people are able to move beyond the worker levels into the realms of being an entrepreneur who gets to 'play'. Moving into the 'play' category is how you begin living in the Entrepreneur Revolution.

THE THREE LEVELS OF 'PLAY'

LEVEL 4: KEY PERSON OF INFLUENCE

When a self-employed person ceases to see themselves as functional and starts seeing themselves as vital they become a 'key person of influence'. In every industry, there are a group of key people whose names come up in conversation, who attract opportunities and who make a lot of money while having fun. Becoming a key person of influence is what's required to break the feeling of work and functionality. It's the first step into the Entrepreneur Revolution.

Key people of influence are clear about their vision, they are credible and they are able to attract resources. They easily attract a team, they can get investors excited, they have more customers than they know how to supply. Best of all, they begin to have fun again!

LEVEL 5: CAMPAIGN-DRIVEN ENTERPRISE

Key people of influence eventually attract opportunities allowing them to tap into larger distribution, leverage on established brands and to align themselves with attractive products.

The fastest way to begin to monetise these sorts of opportunities is with something I call a 'campaign-driven enterprise' (CDE). It's a business that creates a series of exciting promotions, events and launches in order to make the most of the opportunities that seem to keep showing up.

CDEs can make huge amounts of money in the Entrepreneur Revolution. However, they also have a downside. When you take your foot off the accelerator pedal, they slow down very rapidly. The month you stop promoting or launching something you see a sharp decline in your revenues and profits. For this reason, a savvy entrepreneur will move to the next level in the Entrepreneur Revolution.

LEVEL 6: THE GLOBAL SMALL BUSINESS

The global small business (GSB) is the ultimate goal of most entrepreneurs. It's a small to medium-sized business, often with between 5 and 50 people, and it seriously punches above its weight.

It's not linked to geography, it defines itself by an ideology or a philosophy. For that reason, it can trade anywhere and with anyone who shares a similar outlook.

It has well-developed digital assets. It builds a brand within a niche, a bulletproof sales and marketing engine, well-designed systems that automate functional tasks and a dynamic culture that entices high performers to want to stay.

A global small business will not slow down easily, it takes on a life of its own and the challenge is not how to grow it, the challenge is how to direct it as it expands so that it doesn't explode.

As the creator of a global small business you will need to become good at saying no to things that aren't exactly right for your brand. GSBs get opportunities flooding in and if you say yes to too many of them, your GSB will collapse.

Like a racing car driver, you must stay intensely focused on the path ahead and not go thinking about the side streets that might be nice to explore.

Most people would be thrilled to reach this level. As the owner of a GSB you will be known by your peers, you will be affluent, well-travelled and spend most of your time doing things that matter to you. Only after you reach this stage will you fully appreciate why you need to go one step further and why you also had to wait until now to achieve the final level.

There is a final bonus level in the Entrepreneur Revolution where you get to really play a big game.

THE BONUS LEVEL!

LEVEL 7: MAKING A DIFFERENCE ENTERPRISE (MADE)

After building a GSB you will discover that you have influence, money, time and a well-developed sense of purpose and character. You will not be able to resist the thought of leaving a positive legacy and doing something that is meaningful and lasting. You will want to have an impact through your business directly or through politics, the media or your wealth and influence.

After building a GSB you will have the skills, contacts and resources to really do this. Had you attempted it too soon, you would not have been able to do this in a way that felt like your life's purpose. Probably, you would have turned your passion for making a difference into another job.

It would have become functional work and you would end up resenting the very cause you wanted to love. I meet people all the time who try to skip straight to this step out of a deep desire for altruism. They rarely succeed; they end up bitter that they gave so much but barely made a splash.

Even the well-known change makers went through similar steps to the ones I've outlined here. They started as apprentices to other change makers, they did the work, they became key people of influence, they launched their organisations, built a brand and a team and then finally got recognised for making a difference.

Richard Branson's businesses are affected positively by the work of his charity Virgin Unite. His businesses put him in a position to make a difference and the positive work he does in making a difference builds his brand.

When you evolve to a MADE you don't have to sacrifice your own life. People who successfully create a MADE end up having more travel, more fun, more influence, more experiences, more fulfilment and, in many cases, even more money.

As an active entrepreneur who is making a difference, your GSB will benefit enormously.

DON'T SKIP THE LEVELS

Each level is an important part of the journey. As much as you want to get to the higher levels, you will actually move faster towards your goal if you focus on advancing one level at a time.

Yes, this even includes being an apprentice and doing the work so that you understand the functionality of your industry. You don't have to stay at each level for years, or decades, like most people do – but you do need to stamp your foot clearly on the base before moving to the next one.

Remember to keep your eye on the prize. You're living in the most exciting time in history.

There's a renaissance unfolding. The whole world is evolving and reorganising. This is the time for you to make a journey from an industrialised worker to an empowered entrepreneur.

This journey is worth it. As you make the crossing, you will discover yourself becoming a more evolved person, capable of deeper thought, heightened empathy and more inspired decision-making abilities.

You will be capable of achieving the things that, just a few years ago, you thought of as dreams.

Case Study: Growing A Global Small Business

Adrian has been running a web development agency for 13 years. It started when he was asked to redevelop a local tennis centre's website and then the gym across the road wanted a blog set up. A year later, Adrian had a dozen clients and had a designer on the team. Another year passed and the team consisted of four people working on several websites every month.

Fast forward a decade and the business had become more of a job than an exciting business. Adrian had seen several of his clients become very successful with the websites he had built for them. He felt resentment creeping in that he was basically making a wage from the business but it just wasn't scalable.

Adrian needed a fresh perspective so he joined an entrepreneurial network that offered training and collaboration. Being around other entrepreneurs lit a spark inside him again and he started seeing his business very differently. His business was sitting on buckets of potential intellectual property – how had he not seen it before?

Selling his time and services wasn't leading anywhere but he had acquired the skills to create products. He also had worked with enough customers to know a lot about what they struggled with and wanted fixed.

In a facilitated workshop he mapped out several product ideas and showed some of his peers. Their reactions fuelled even more excitement.

Adrian put a landing page up for his new software solution and invited people to join a waiting list. Over 700 people had registered by the time his beta version was ready. He surveyed his clients and discovered they were happy to pay around $1800 per year for his software solution.

Adrian launched a beta group of clients who got a free trial and then paid $150 per month. Three months after the launch the feedback was looking great and new clients had started signing up, many of whom were not even in the same country. It was a shock one day when a new client based in Slovenia signed up to the software.

The business grew and Adrian signed up the 1000th paying client within two years of launch. This was the moment he could completely do away with all remaining website development clients and focus 100% on his software business. He then added a training programme to support clients and this really took things to a new level. Then he launched a podcast covering success stories and innovative ways to use the software. By year three he had crossed 2000 paying clients producing $300,000 per month of revenue that easily paid for his team of 10 people.

Adrian started travelling more often because he could work from anywhere. When he travelled, he would get in touch with his clients and record a podcast with them. He noticed that he was more productive when he worked in a flexible way, so he got rid of the office and gave the extra money to his employees to work from home or wherever they chose.

Adrian realised that he loved the business being focused and lean. He didn't want to build a massive business with investors or large debts so he decided to keep his team to just 10 passionate and skilled people. The team used basic software tools to communicate and they kept meetings and administration to a minimum. Adrian implemented special bonuses based on consistent profitability and customer delight and the business developed a much loved brand with healthy margins.

Through the creation of great products and a vibrant small team, everyone was enjoying the benefits of having a global small business.

CHAPTER 7

THREE MINDSETS FOR AN AI-ENABLED WORLD

In the current economy, every business will need to reinvent itself multiple times per decade. The mother of all disruptive technologies has finally arrived and is set to be more impactful than the Internet was in the early 2000s.

For a fraction of the labour cost, AI can create images, video, code and text that highly paid professionals were required for just a few years ago. This technology is going to do much of the work lawyers, doctors, engineers, architects, animators, editors, auditors, accountants and developers were doing. It's going to do this ubiquitously at a marginal cost. This change will transform every industry, everywhere in the world. Rapidly.

Artificial intelligence is the next great general purpose technology that will completely reshape the economy and civilisation as we know it. Steam engines, railways, steel, factory lines, standardised parts, combustion engines and oil were the general purpose technologies of the industrial age.

Data, software, the Internet and now AI are the building blocks of the world we are entering.

Before Issac Singer invented his mass-produced sewing machine a dress shirt took 14 hours to produce by a tailor – this dropped to around an hour with a sewing machine and the level of skill required dropped precipitously too.

Things we once believed to be the time-consuming domain of experts are going to be made simple and fast with AI. Legal contracts, medical procedures, financial reporting, website development, engineering and architecture will all be fast and easy – you'll ask the AI using natural language and it will create what you want almost instantaneously.

This means the skills that made you valuable in the past will not make you valuable in the future. A fine tailor could try to justify spending 14 hours making a shirt but the majority of people simply won't spend the money for this imperceivable difference.

There are three mindset shifts that we must all make in order to be valuable in a post-AI world: vitality versus functionality; context versus content; and creating versus consuming.

VITALITY VERSUS FUNCTIONALITY

Functionality is defined as performing a set of tasks or processes efficiently. Vitality is different. There are two literal definitions of the word 'vital' – the first is 'irreplaceable' and the second is 'life-force'.

Money, wealth, power and influence move towards people who are the 'irreplaceable life-force' in their domain.

The people who aren't easy to get rid of, the ones who can't be forgotten; these are the people who truly make it. In a world with AI and robotics, all of the functionality will be automated. The work that will remain will look a lot more like play.

Telling stories, bringing things to life, capturing people's attention, using wit, humour, irreverence and spark are valuable skills now.

To become valuable we must automate ourselves up not out. There are countless books and seminars available today that focus on automating and systemising what you do. They tell you to avoid putting your personality into your business because then the business will become dependent on you.

They say you shouldn't get too known in your field or else people will want to deal with you personally. They say you should build the business so it doesn't need you.

I agree that you should not be doing functional tasks that could be automated or systemised. However, I believe the purpose of getting these tasks taken care of is so you can become even more vital to your business – more irreplaceable and more of a life-force.

Your goal is to move to higher and greater levels of irreplaceability.

People who are functional end up being replaced; people who are vital end up with ownership. They stay true to their centre and they own their space. Often, this results in them owning their marketplace, their business and their niche too.

Vital people have a sense of curiosity, a spark, a contagious energy and a genuine desire to serve at a new higher standard.

Recently, I watched a documentary about the legendary hair stylist, Vidal Sassoon. Everyone he met described him as a true artist. He cared about hair; he wasn't satisfied unless he gave it his all.

He studied architecture for inspiration. He danced around the person in the chair as he styled them. You could never tell him the haircut you wanted. Instead he would study your face and tell you what haircut he would do for you.

Vidal Sassoon became a very, very rich man. He didn't try to retire from hairdressing, he tried to find ways to impact even more people and to get into it deeper than anyone else. He was vital.

My friend Cathy Burke is the CEO of the Hunger Project Australia. She brings so much life to that organisation that people can't help but get involved. Under her commitment it's gone from annual revenues of a few hundred thousand dollars into the millions; and it's still climbing.

She has put in place lots of systems and best practices but only for one reason; she wants all the boring stuff taken care of so her team can spend more time and energy being engaged with the cause.

Great entrepreneurs don't use systems, technology and best practices to get out of their business. They use them to get in deeper.

Vital people don't dream of retiring some day. In fact, they think about ways that they can keep doing more of what they love to do for as long as they can.

Both Rupert Murdoch and Warren Buffet are examples of billionaires who chose to work growing their businesses well into their 90s without giving a thought to retirement.

I could make a list of almost every billionaire in the world who is in 'retirement age' and almost every single one of them still shows up to work!

But, of course, it isn't work. When it feels like work you want to retire, you want to knock off early, you need other hobbies to keep you sane and you are dreaming of going on holidays.

What you are actually dreaming of is being in a space of vitality. You are dreaming of what it would be like to wake up excited about what the day could offer you and doing things that make you feel even more invigorated than when you started. You yearn to be the life force.

Well, here is the amazingly good news. You live in a world where you have vast options and can do almost anything your heart desires!

You can create things, you can be a public speaker, you can trade things, you can invent things, you can bring people together; and any of that stuff could make you wealthy and fulfil your dreams.

Before you read on, do you agree or not? Every day, isn't the world showing you fresh new examples of people who are fully embracing life and making millions?

Are you seeing examples of people who hate their boring, replaceable life but at least they get paid fortunes? I'm not. I only see people who are leaning into their lives and getting the real rewards.

The truth about retirement is that you will dream about the days you were most engaged in life's meaningful work, or you will wish you had been.

Talk to any elderly person and they will tell you to quit trying to do something you hate for the money. They will tell you to go out and do something that inspires you while you still have time to do something great.

If you were in a vital space when you were creating your income wouldn't you certainly make more income? People would notice you more and want to do business with you more. It's time to give up on the dream of 'passive income', 'easy wins' and a 'comfortable retirement'. It's time to say: 'I will only do things I never want to retire from and I will do these things in a way that adds value to others and tangibly rewards me as well.'

Wealth flows to vital people, not functional people. Wealth flows to people who build a reputation and a profile. Wealth flows to people who acknowledge their luck and go out to create more of it.

When you are ready for the next steps to becoming more vital, known and lucky please turn the page. We're about to turn your passion into a meaningful, profitable empire that helps other people.

CONTEXT VERSUS CONTENT

Large Language Models (LLMs) power generative AI. These LLMs are created by feeding the AI with every available piece of content available. By the time an LLM comes into existence it has read every Wikipedia page, legal document, magazine article, book review, news story and academic paper known to man. In its digital brain is practically the whole Internet just waiting to be discussed.

There's a problem though; if you don't ask it a question it just sits there silently minding its business. An LLM doesn't have any goals and it doesn't know what to do with all of its knowledge. It needs you to guide it towards an aim.

You need to provide the context so that it can give you the useful content.

Imagine you have a clear goal. You want to raise money for your startup. Armed with that context the AI can spit out the steps to take to raise angel funding. It can write the emails you will use to approach an investor, the investor memorandum and business plan. It will help you script your pitch. It will produce a shareholders agreement and a deed of adherence. It will advise on various tax incentives and provide the steps for setting up a data-room before you onboard your new investors.

AI is like a bright employee waiting for the boss to give it a job to do.

In the industrial age, having content in your head was a valuable resource. What made a doctor, engineer, accountant or other expert valuable was the content locked up in their head. Now that content is freely available to anyone who knows what to ask for — or more importantly has a reason for asking.

An engineer is in the habit of waiting to be asked for content. They like to be given a challenge to solve. When

Elon Musk walks into the room and sets them the challenge of creating reusable rockets for getting humans to Mars, the engineers jolt to attention and get to work.

The big challenge for every engineer now is to find their own purpose that will serve as their own contextual marker. It will be more valuable to spot the problem worth solving than to know solutions to problems that have already been solved.

The masters of the game are those who have defined the game. As soon as that context is clear, the speed that you can access the building blocks of your vision is becoming insanely fast.

Context comes from finding your purpose. Everyone needs a why more than ever to act as their compass.

Your Inner Compass

In the age of AI, you must have an inner compass that guides you. This is the context for your own life. Without this inner compass, you will be chewed up and spat out. AIs will find ways to distract you and send you down endless rabbit holes.

With an inner compass, you will be able to ignore the temptations of endless scrolling, video games and gadgets. You'll only engage with things that align to your own purpose.

Roman Emperor Marcus Aurelius was the most powerful man in the world in his time. He could have had any earthy desire fulfilled. If he had wanted a city destroyed he need only ask. If he desired endless food, sex or entertainment it would have been given to him.

This is not how the famous stoic emperor chose to use his power. He was on a journey to define and engage in meaningful struggles that would align him more deeply to his highest values. He turned his back on the gluttony and excess available to an emperor and walked a path of wisdom, courage, temperance and justice.

In the age of AI, we find ourselves in the same conundrum as this great man. We will have endless opportunities to fulfil our carnal desires but we must each rise above this and pursue something of more meaning. In hyper-realistic digital worlds there are no rules. You can simulate any experience you want in a meta verse somewhere and you can organise almost anything you want in the real world.

You will need to create context for your business and your life. You'll have to take time to think about and define the goals you want to pursue, meaningful struggles you want to endure, boundaries you want to uphold and the moral code you enforce upon yourself and your associates.

CREATING VERSUS CONSUMING

Artificial intelligence has two superpowers in the way it interacts with humans. It has the power to get us to consume more than we intended and the power to get us to create more than we could.

When someone doom-scrolls for hours on social media, AI has used its powers to make you hyper-consume. You only wanted to quickly check the app and as if by magic you found yourself hooked with captivating content. Behind the scenes, the AI had built a model of your browsing behaviour and it tested thousands of pieces of content on your digital twin to discover what you are most likely to respond to. While you are watching one carefully selected 15-second video, it's running another thousand experiments in the background to choose what it will show you next.

AI is often given a game to play where the goal is to get you to buy more, listen to more, binge watch, game for longer, endlessly snack and generally over-consume the things AI is tasked to promote.

AI will not lose this game. If it can beat the best chess players at their game it sure as hell knows how to keep you glued to your screen. The only way to beat it is to create an air-gap on your devices – you have to remove the apps from your phone so you can free up that time to create something of value.

AI can help you to create more than you ever dreamed possible. Using advanced tools, you can make videos, podcasts, assessments, art, research papers, products and software at warp speed. You can literally speak your ideas into existence and achieve things in an hour that would have taken an expert 14 hours to create just a decade ago.

In the near future a wedge will be driven through society that separates the AI-empowered haves from the AI-distracted have-nots. You do not want to be on the wrong side of this wedge. There will come a point where it becomes too late – the consumers will have fallen too far behind the makers. They will be kept busy with games and entertainment and miss out on the real joy of life.

The experience of building something that gets talked about is often the most rewarding and energetically uplifting thing you'll ever do.

Better yet, the results of having a remarkable business can be staggering. You don't just make wages, you make profits. You don't just help your clients, you blow their minds and make a difference to their lives! You don't just get a pat on the back, you get people raving about you!

There's little joy in the endless cycle of trying to come up with the 'easy money-making idea'. There's loads of joy in pushing something to be truly a stand-out.

Everything you consume requires energy – either to digest it, or to maintain it in your life.

Creating is opposite. When you create, energy flows through you. The act of creating wakes you up and makes you feel joyous.

If you don't believe me, go and look at the Forbes Rich List of self-made billionaires. Hardly any of them are retired. Almost none of them have used their wealth to lean back from life and sit on a beach endlessly consuming stuff. Most of them are typically engaged in the joy of creating, not the burden of consuming.

Steve Jobs was diagnosed with cancer but chose to spend his final years pouring himself into the act of creating. He could have chosen to do literally anything. No one would have judged him harshly if he chose to retire. Why did he stay in the game? Because creating is joyous. Leaning in is joyful.

Contrast Steve Jobs to the majority of lotto winners. It's a widely known statistical fact that most lotto winners become depressed and unhappy. They suddenly have the power to rapidly consume everything they ever dreamed of; and it sucks the life out of them.

For starters, the mere fact that they bought a lotto ticket shows you they were leaning back on life, looking for an exit. They then get the money and they go out to consume. Everything they buy comes with obligations to maintain it or digest it. It's exhausting and there's no joy in it.

Many people have fond memories of their college years. They were broke, they hardly owned a stick of furniture, they had to forage for money from under the sofa just to buy lunch, but they still remember this as a great time in their life. The reason people loved their college years was because they weren't weighed down with stuff, they were busy creating all the time and they didn't have the means to consume.

College, for most people, was a time when they had to invent their identity but, for some reason, people stop.

Keep doing it, keep reinventing yourself, keep creating.

CREATE THE FUTURE, DON'T CONSUME THE PAST

Don't fantasise about going back to the past as there's simply no such thing as 'going back to the way things were'. Life doesn't move backwards, it moves forward. There's no time machine coming to pick you up. You are not going back to your college years, the great year you had in 2003, or the good old pre-recession days. You are moving forward in time and the only way things will be better is if you create them as better.

Let me share a typical example of what happens when you try to go back in time. I once spontaneously went on an amazing holiday with friends to a place we'd never been before. Without much planning we had to invent the trip as we travelled and we created the experiences on the go. We discovered unique places, we found ourselves in surprising and humorous situations, we met interesting people we didn't expect to meet. It turned out to be amazing and, the following year, we tried to do it again by going back to the same place and attempting to do the same things.

Create!   Consume!

When we got there it was not as fun. We tried to recreate 'spontaneously meeting those hilarious people' and they weren't there. We attempted to revisit that 'magical spot where everything just clicked' and it just didn't click.

It never works out trying to 'get back' to the past; you can't do it.

Why didn't it happen? Because we were approaching the experience as a consumer. We were trying to consume an experience of the past rather than create something right now.

Let go of consuming the past. Let go of trying to 'get back' to any place.

If you want more joy, stop consuming. Stop consuming people, things or events and stop trying to 'get back' the past. Start creating the future. Reinvent yourself constantly, based on who you want to be.

CONSUMING IS A DRAIN, CREATING IS JOY

Now let's apply this to everyday life. It's time to stop reading books and write your own book. Stop attending events, plan your own event. Stop reading the news, start creating something newsworthy. Don't go looking for answers, start answering questions for others. Stop buying products, start creating your own products to deliver to the world.

Stop waiting for the right time, start creating the space for magic to happen.

When you replace your entire day with acts of creation, you will have energy. When you fill your day with acts of consumption you will burn out.

LEAN IN TO DISRUPTION

On a snowboard, it's common to feel tired, unstable, stuck, or out of your depth. Most newbie riders naturally lean back to try to escape the situation that's troubling them.

They secretly wish they were off the mountain or they wish they were on a nicer run. However, the minute you don't want to be where you are you lean back, your feet wobble, you can't steer yourself and you find yourself face down in the snow. Leaning back causes you to lose balance. It hurts, it's humiliating, and it makes you want to get the hell off the mountain even more.

Experienced riders know that leaning back doesn't work. They know that if they want to have a good time they must overcome the urge to lean back. They must lean *in* to the mountain.

As soon as they lean in, they get stability, control and they get into the flow of things.

Most people are leaning back from their business, industry, job or even their life. Especially when disruption comes along.

Secretly they are wanting things to be easier. They want to wait and see what happens before they act. They have ideas but they want it to be easy and risk free to implement them. This isn't how it works.

Entrepreneurs must implement with excellence in all terrains, not when it's easy.

Leaning back in your business or your life will cost you dearly in this moment of AI disruption.

Leaning back is when you start looking for an exit strategy before your business is genuinely valuable; it's when you want an old product just to keep on selling even when AI has clearly changed things; it's when you get annoyed that you have competition who have innovated when you didn't. Leaning back is the lazy way, or the way of a coward.

Successful entrepreneurs lean in when disruption comes. When they have the chance to invest money in a smarter way, they take it. If a great person becomes available they hire them. If a competitor shows up, they get fired up for the challenge of outperforming them.

When you lean in, you don't dream of retirement. You don't hope for an unexpected exit to show up. You hope to face even bigger challenges, you want your vision to show up faster and you dream of *never* retiring.

Leaning in means working with the best people, it means showing up with your game face on and leaving your doubts at the door.

Leaning in means taking the calculated risk, it means committing to being excellent, and to doing what it takes to solve whatever problems come along. It means spending time, money and energy when the opportunity comes along and then taking accountability for the results.

Leaning in is about pursuing your vision, loving your customers, developing your team, caring about the details and committing to getting it right.

Leaning in is about wishing to be better, not wishing for things to be easier.

Strangely, leaning in produces an easier life.

Just like on a snowboard, when you lean in life gets easier. When you lean in, your business works, you attract a great team, your products sell. When you lean out, life is hard. When you lean in, life shows up as easy, you have stability and you attract opportunity.

In the years ahead, there will be winners and losers due to disruption. Your best chance at being a winner in the age of AI is to lean in to this disruption.

CHAPTER 8

THE VERY ESSENCE
OF YOUR SUCCESS

You've shifted your mindset, created a product ecosystem and built a team. You are surfing the waves of disruption and leaning in You're doing everything right but will you succeed? What is it that makes some people successful while others struggle?

Why is it that some people in an industry are millionaires and other people in the same industry are just getting by? What will really make the difference between your success or failure?

Why is Kendal Jenner paid millions to be a model, while other models, who are just as pretty, get paid $400 a day?

Why is Ed Sheeran a millionaire singer/songwriter when others only make enough for their next meal, despite performing their heart out day in, day out?

Why does Philippe Stark get paid millions to design interiors and other interior designers make basic hourly wages?

I have three answers to this riddle but, before I tell you the first reason, make a list of all the traits you think the successful people have that the others don't.

Make a list of all the things that you think separate the highly valued and highly paid people from those just getting by. What do you think are the mystery ingredients that got them where they are today?

_____   _____

_____   _____

_____   _____

NOTE: *Don't read on until you have listed your answers.*

I hope you thought of a few things before reading on. In fact, if you haven't, please do so. You'll get more out of this book if you do.

If you are like most people you will put down words such as self-belief, determination, passion, hard work, leadership skills and decisiveness.

Great words but they all have a bit of a problem. They are not mutually exclusive.

I can take all those sorts of words and put them next to a list of the richest people on the planet and we would find, sure enough, these words are relevant to them. These super success stories have courage, determination, passion, and all those things we mentioned.

The problem is, when I take those same traits and apply them to people who aren't so successful, I can find those qualities too. I can witness determination in the eyes of the Uber Driver who works 70 hours a week; I can see belief in the network marketer who thrusts their sample pack into the hands of another unwilling contact; I can find plenty of passion in the kids' entertainer who arrives at another 8-year-old's party.

It is the same list of traits, but some people are wildly successful while others aren't.

So what is the real key to success long term? What are the things that set all the big-time people apart from the small-time strugglers? What is the thing that, if the little guys had it, they would make it? The thing that all the big guys acknowledge and the little guys fail to think about?

There are three keys that all successful entrepreneurs possess and that you will need on your journey if you want to make it big – luck, reputation and leverage.

THE FIRST KEY: LUCK

You're probably thinking, 'Luck . . . you mean I read all this stuff to arrive at the key to big success and it's LUCK!'

Sorry to say this, but luck is going to play a part in your life whether you like it or not. Hard work is not going to be your unique selling proposition, you simply couldn't work hard enough.

Your big break isn't going to come through more belief in yourself – just watch *American Idol* and you will see plenty of people with belief, passion and courage who get turned down. Yep, the bad news is that *all* successful people have been wildly lucky!

The good news is that you are already born lucky. If you are reading this book, you had an education, you have money to buy books, you have time to read.

The other piece of good news is that you can cultivate luck. There are lucky places and unlucky places. There are lucky people to associate with and unlucky people you should avoid.

You also might not even see just how much luck is already showing up for you and has been showing up for you since the moment you were born.

The first key to luck is that you learn to recognise luck. If you can't even see how lucky you are already you will be blind to any good fortune that shows up in the future.

Here's how I discovered my luck.

I had just finished giving a talk over breakfast to about 100 wealthy Indian business owners at one of the most luxurious hotels in Mumbai, India.

Afterwards, the organiser asked me if I wanted to meet her friend, who ran a school in the slum area of Mumbai, and I enthusiastically accepted the offer not really knowing what I was in store for.

We caught a cab into the heart of the slum area. This wasn't just a few people doing it tough, this was millions of people living on top of each other; each person desperately seeking a better life, each struggling for survival without what I would consider the basics of clean water, electricity and a solid roof to sleep under.

I ventured into the school and met with a class of 40 vibrant students. The tin shed classroom was a sweltering sauna. Yet the kids were so eager to learn. They scribed out their alphabets with broken chalk on their slate. They listened enthusiastically to their teacher and they graciously accepted me being in their class.

Their clothes were little more than rags, probably thrown out by someone in the West for having a small rip or stain; now they were the only set of clothes these kids had.

As my day of touring ended, I got back into a taxi and headed to my next hotel. My cab crawled along in peak traffic and, with no air conditioning, the sweat rolled down my face. I sat for two hours, staring at scene after scene of poverty.

At one point, the cab passed an aid agency dumping barrels of clean water on the road, and dozens of people swarmed in to fill their drinking containers. One little boy, who must have been barely five years old, pushed a rusty tin can under the stream and gladly drank from it. It broke my heart to watch.

Then, after what seemed like hours in the cab, we rounded a corner to my five-star hotel, where the guards waved us through the gates.

On the other side were beautiful water features. Innumerable gallons of clean, drinkable water flowed from fountains and statues, sprinklers kept the pristine gardens green and a waterfall churned down an artificial rock face into the pools.

Although it was nothing I hadn't seen before, on this day I felt my heart tearing up just looking at it.

Emotional and overheated, I checked into the hotel. The receptionist recognised I was a speaker at the conference and offered me an upgrade. I was ushered to a 'superior room' that was about four times the size of the school I'd just been in.

This was all becoming too much. I figured I'd better shower and cool off. As I turned the shower on, four water jets came to life and so did my eyes.

Tears streamed down my face. I had felt so closely connected to the children in the school, so welcomed and so happy to be with them. Now I was set in a scene that would be beyond their wildest dreams.

What's worse is that this wasn't a new scene for me. It was just another five-star hotel, cut and pasted like any other I'd stayed in on my travels.

In that moment, I discovered my luck. For the first time ever my eyes were open to how, every moment of my life, I had been living one of the luckiest lives in the history of humanity.

It suddenly hit me: I have water, education, food, housing and access to technology.

I have film makers spending millions to create entertainment for me on the off chance I might watch it. I have airlines running fleets of planes around the world on the off chance I want to fly. I have farmers preparing their best produce and sending it to stores that are minutes from my front door.

I live in such a lucky time in history! Never before could people get their questions answered in seconds. Never in history could people communicate their ideas with so many others. Never has there been more finance, more resources, more exciting conversations.

Whichever way I look at it, I'm living a life more extravagant than the royal families throughout the ages. King Louis XIV would sit talking to me with his jaw open in amazement of what I have access to in my day-to-day life.

When all that really hit me I truly got it. 'I'm so lucky!' This realisation allowed me to see luck more easily at every turn in my life. Accepting that I am lucky, opened me up to more of it.

I am lucky; and so are you.

If you can't start with that, you will miss the luck that shows up next. The ability to acknowledge how lucky you already are, and to be grateful for it, allows you to see opportunities more clearly.

YOU CAN MAKE YOURSELF LUCKIER

Once you recognise how lucky you already are, the next step is to learn how to influence luck. You can coax it into your life and encourage it to show up.

You influence your luck when you show up in places that are luckier, when you spend time with people who are luckier, when you learn ideas that produce luck, when you get crystal clear on your vision and when you begin having lucky conversations.

Given the choice between doing another repetitive day at the office or going to an event that's full of inspired leaders, I will choose the event. It's luckier.

I don't know who I will meet or what will come of it but I do know that there's a good chance that something great will happen.

Given the choice of talking to someone who's convinced there are no opportunities out there, or talking to someone who's enthusing about an exciting future, I will talk to the person with an inspired outlook. It's luckier.

I don't know what exactly I will learn from them, I just know that I will probably discover something worth knowing about.

Given the choice between watching random TV or listening to a riveting audiobook I will choose the book. It's luckier.

Playing a mindless computer game isn't as lucky as meditating. Avoiding people isn't as lucky as talking to strangers. Ignoring customer complaints isn't luck but taking a disgruntled customer out for coffee to learn what went wrong is.

Every day we are making choices that will either make us even luckier, or choices that repel the luck that is desperately trying to show up in our lives.

People want to be able to create success the same way a chef makes a pie. They want a recipe and a formula. They want to know what exactly to do in a step-by-step method.

Unfortunately, a huge part of the formula is that you have to be lucky. The good news is that being lucky is actually something you are more in control of than you might think. Luck is already trying to beat down your door.

THE SECOND KEY: REPUTATION

We are moving into a time when everyone and everything is connected. In the Entrepreneur Revolution your most prized asset is your personal brand and reputation.

When somebody Googles your name, the first page of results is a clear indication of how the world sees you.

Is it clear what you do? Is it clear what you are good at? Can people see a photo or a video of you? Can they find testimonials? This is important stuff.

In a world where the most cutting-edge technology has been designed to leverage your message, you must build a profile and guard your reputation.

We live in a world where your reputation will follow you around for life. One seriously stupid decision will be searchable for a very long time if the story hits the Internet.

Damaging his reputation cost Tiger Woods over $25m in lost contracts in the short term and $100m in career earnings. It's an extreme example illustrating a point that's relevant at all levels of business. Your reputation matters – don't roll the dice with it.

Warren Buffet says: 'It can take 20 years to build a reputation and 5 minutes to ruin it. If you think about that, you'll do things differently.'

On the flip side, a great reputation will pick you up when you're down or even rescue your business. Richard

Branson's reputation is so strong, his involvement in the failing bank Northern Rock helped to turn it around.

He says: 'Your reputation is all you have in life – your personal reputation and the reputation of your brand. And if you do anything that damages that reputation, you can destroy your company.'

My first book, *Key Person of Influence*, discussed how I witnessed certain people become go-to people in their industry. These people then earned more money, had more fun and attracted more opportunity.

My first book became a best-seller. As a result, I was featured in the media and was offered considerable amounts of money just to turn up and speak at events around the world. Often, I would get paid more money for a 45-minute talk than most people earn in a month.

I've been offered shares in other people's businesses because of my reputation and my profile.

As a result of my reputation and profile, I was approached by a major publisher to write the book you have in your hands.

So, a reputation and a profile are valuable assets that pay regular dividends. People who have a reputation receive inbound opportunities. Their phone rings every day with perfect projects. They don't have to chase constantly for their next payment, the money comes and finds them.

By far your most prized asset must be your reputation. It's an asset that will pay you well for life. Guard it, nurture it, make decisions with your reputation in mind because great entrepreneurs believe that money comes and goes but your reputation is permanent.

Consider all the people you know who make great money, who live exciting lives, who have influence and success in abundance. Unless they inherited it, I can guarantee you that they are well known in their field.

Their names come up in conversation, they hear about opportunities first, they earn more and they have more fun doing it – they have made a name for themselves in their industry and the rewards show up in volumes.

If you do the things that impact your reputation in a positive way you will attract more opportunities. These opportunities create wealth and success.

Never has there been a better time in history to make a name for yourself. New technology and the widespread sharing of resources make it easier than ever to do all five of the steps listed above.

No need to look for some special secret to wealth. The secret is: you are already standing on a mountain of value but you need to let the world know about it. After you've made a name for yourself, expect to see more opportunity, more fun, more inbound enquiries and even a lot more money.

If you put more focus into building your reputation, enhancing your brand and making a name for yourself in your industry, you'll always have a valuable asset.

NOTE: *Take the Key Person of Influence Scorecard and measure your ability to influence in a business context. It offers powerful ways to boost your reputation. Visit* https:// scorecard.dent.globa

THE THIRD KEY: LEVERAGE

Big success requires your value to multiply across some form of leverage. If a product is stocked on the shelves of every Walmart, it's going to make a lot of money. If a new app is featured on the AppStore it will start selling. If a celebrity endorses your brand, it will build the brand faster. If a venture capital firm invests in your tech company you can afford to do the things an unfunded company dreams of.

You don't have enough time to build something of value as well as build up the leverage you need to take it out to a lot of people. You have to gain access to someone else's leverage.

The leverage you will need can't be available to everyone though – it has to be a rare and protected form of leverage that most people can't access. It must be kept behind a big gate.

YouTube offers awesome leverage to creators but there's no gate – anyone can upload videos to the platform. Amazon lets almost anyone put a book on the Kindle Store, Spotify will host almost anyone's podcast and anyone is free to use ChatGPT or Google when they like. Even though these are all awesome forms of leverage, they are accessible to everyone and therefore offer no special advantage on their own.

The gated forms of leverage are hard to achieve but they unlock a massive advantage. Things like celebrity endorsements, venture capital, distribution deals, genuine mentoring, access to unique data or insights are all gated forms of leverage. They are not a guarantee of success but they will put you into a new category and larger-scale success will be far more likely.

In many ways, the reason you work so hard and build a reputation is to qualify to access rare and protected forms of leverage – to get past the gatekeepers. Plenty of people work hard and keep their reputations clean but don't succeed and this is often because they didn't reach out and attempt to access the special advantages they could have been granted.

At some point in your career you will need to reach out and ask for access for leverage that few people are granted access to. It's possible that you might be discovered randomly but it's unlikely. The people who control access to leverage are spoiled for choice. They have countless people reaching out to them each year so they do not often run around looking for people to discover.

Rejection will be part of the process. The first time you reach out to a celebrity to discuss an endorsement deal, you will probably not hear back from them. This isn't a no, this is a not this time.

For you to gain access you will need to be doing something special, something scalable and something that doesn't present additional risk. You'll need a good reputation, you'll need to have put in the work to be ready for the rocket launch they can offer you. Normally they'll need to see how you've handled smaller deals before them. The breakthrough moment will normally not feel like a big deal, it will feel like something you are ready for.

When the gate opens and you gain access to the raw power of leverage, be ready to take off. You are probably going to achieve more in the year ahead than you achieved in the previous decade.

LIVING THE DREAM

There is one final change that will allow you to live the dream and enjoy the great opportunities of the Entrepreneur Revolution. You have to learn to lead with your heart open.

In the Industrial Revolution, humans were seen to be part of the machinery. The system was designed to dehumanise workers, to get them to tune out from their inner calling and to get on with whatever tasks they had been assigned.

As a result, many people forgot what it was to be human. In the Western world, we detuned from our humanity to such a great extent that it's probably no coincidence that epidemics of depression have affected millions of people.

A big part of the Entrepreneur Revolution is rediscovering your humanity. At the core of the Entrepreneur Revolution is love.

Let's discuss why the Entrepreneur Revolution is powered by it.

This may sound very soppy and unbusinesslike, but nothing could be further from the truth. It's actually very logical, practical and real. If love is missing from your business, your business will not survive in the future.

You must love what you do, your team must love working in your business, your clients must love buying from you and your community must love having your business within it.

To explore how massive this trend is, let's go back in time.

THE AGE OF 'HANDS'

For thousands of years, humanity thrived because of our hands. Humans developed dexterity and we became brilliant tool makers.

We could precisely move objects in such a way that we could shape the world to our will.

We made weapons that could take down a mighty wildebeest. We made ploughs that could turn a dry patch of land into a fertile crop. We developed looms that could make warm cloths and shield us from the elements.

The most admired men in society were those who were strong with their arms and precise with their aim. Kings were judged on their prowess with a sword and leaders were elected because of their skills in battle.

No other animal on earth could compete with our ability to move objects so precisely and we became the most dominant species on earth as a result.

In the 1500s, the Renaissance celebrated human dexterity by producing fine art. Our precision had evolved to a point that Michelangelo fashioned the mighty David from stone, with his gaze mesmerising and his form considered perfect.

The 'age of hands' took us right up until the dawn of the Industrial Revolution when something very strange happened: we created machines that could beat us at our own game.

THE AGE OF 'HEADS'

The machines we built in the Industrial Revolution super-seded our own dexterity. One industrial sewing machine could outperform a dozen fine tailors, one tractor could outperform one hundred diligent farmers, one engine could outperform one thousand strong men.

What happened, as a result, was a huge displacement of workers. Unemployment went through the roof as technology removed the need for thousands of well-trained hands.

Then came the thinking men. Carnegie, with his ingenious Bessemer Steel Process; Rockefeller with his standardised distribution model for oil; JP Morgan with his financial weapons of mass acquisition; Onassis with his new type of oil tankers.

Suddenly, the most powerful men on earth were not particularly talented with their hands, they were brilliant with their minds. They could out-think their opponents.

First came the strategists. Rockefeller rethought the way oil was distributed. Carnegie rethought the steel-making process. Morgan rethought financial products. Onassis rethought the way oil was shipped internationally.

Then came the second round big thinkers. Along came Sam Walton with his Wal-Mart megastores, Ingvar Kamprad with his IKEA furniture, Bill Gates with his Microsoft operating systems and Larry Ellison with his Oracle databases.

The age of heads meant the highest-paid people on earth were thinkers. Lawyers, accountants, scientists, company directors, managers and CEOs became the leaders in our society.

The age of heads – or the 'information age' or the 'ideas economy' – produced wild new innovations that transformed humanity and humanity's place in the world.

Then, once more, something strange happened. We built machines that could beat us at our own game for a second time: we created computers.

The 'age of heads' took us right up until the dawn of the Entrepreneur Revolution (now) when something very strange happened again.

THE AGE OF 'HEARTS'

One piece of software could do the work of one hundred accountants, one website could do the work of one hundred managers, one automated system could outperform one hundred scientists. Artificial intelligence has read every book, research paper, manual and blog and it can use that knowledge to create things better than 90% of experts in many fields.

Just as machines became better than us at dexterity, computers are now better than us at thinking.

At the same time a new type of technology emerged, the technology of intimacy.

Intimacy is about knowing what someone else is experiencing. It's about knowing what you are thinking, what you are feeling, what you've seen, what you've heard, what you've tasted and smelled. It's about knowing who you are friends with, who you like, what you like and what interests you. It's about sharing – everything.

Does that sound familiar? It should – it's the biggest business in town now.

Social networks and social media were born as a way to share our experiences of life.

Through the act of sharing and caring and liking and discussing we've seen multibillion dollar businesses created in just a few short years.

It's not just the Mark Zuckerbergs of the world who are making money. All over the world, people are running their small businesses and discovering the effect of using social media and social networks.

If you care about your clients, listen to them, talk to them and share experiences with them. Treat them like you would treat a friend and you will find your business is booming.

The new game is love.

The companies that will do well in the future are the ones that discuss love in the boardroom.

They will ask questions such as:

> How would we build this business in a way that people love working with us, love shopping with us, love supplying us, love talking about us and love to see us doing well?

Talking about growing sales, beating the competition and dominating the market will not get any of those things achieved. Talking about 'love' will.

Love is about passion, love is about care, love is about intimacy, love is about . . . love.

There are going to be tough times ahead as people make this change. Countless men were put out of work because their hands were no longer needed and their heads were not trained for the ideas economy. Likewise, countless people will be put out of work because their heads are no longer needed and their hearts haven't been trained for the entrepreneur economy.

Just like 'hands people' would have rejected the concept of an 'ideas economy', we will see many 'heads people' rejecting the concept of a 'passion economy'.

Just as there was turbulence during the transition into the industrial economy, there will be turbulence as we transition into the entrepreneurship economy.

The good news is that you now know what you have to do, and I think you will like it because your job in the *new* economy is to love what you do. Sharing your love of something with others is what makes you valuable.

All of the doing innovation has been done for you in the form of low-cost manufacturing and distribution options. All the thinking innovation has been done for you in the form of readily available software solutions and AI. All that is left for you to do is to come into your industry with more love than anyone else.

You need to care about the customer experience (which might even start by calling them something other than a 'customer'). You need to become more connected with what people in your industry are thinking and feeling. You must learn to talk openly about why others might love being part of your vision. You must share stories, energise people with your passion and enrol them into your connected community.

The pay-off is huge. Can you imagine waking up every day and getting paid to do what you love? Can you imagine hearing back from people who say you delivered real value to them and, because of that, they simply love to do business with you?

Can you imagine living in the entrepreneur sweet spot? You do what you are passionate about. You deliver amazing value. You get paid well for it.

. . . and everyone loves you for it.

For the first time in history this isn't just a dream for a few, it's a reality for millions.

Money won't make you happy, being skilled won't make you happy, knowing your passion won't make you happy.

Combining all three of these things will leave you feeling over the moon!

I live my life in this sweet spot. It blows my mind some days just how lucky I am. I travel, I earn amazing money and my clients report back to me that they love doing business with us.

I want you to know that if you aren't quite there yet, keep leaning in. Keep going. The juice *is* worth the squeeze.

It's going to be worth it. You're going to make it. You're living in the most amazing time to be alive and you're reading this book for a reason.

For whatever reason, you were born into these times. You could have been born at any other time or place in history and your battle would have been with disease, hunger or conflict.

Any other time in history and you wouldn't have had a voice or a platform to share your message. Any other time in history and your ideas would live and die in your head without seeing the light of day.

Who knows why, but here you are living in a time when anything is possible, where you do have a voice, where your ideas can come to life and where you can empower yourself and others through enterprise.

You're here in the right time and the right place in history to make a difference and to live out your own fairytale.

Don't waste a day. These revolutionary times don't come around often. Seize this day today as your moment.

Put down this book and become the person you dreamed you would be.

Let the world be your playground as you embrace your role in the Entrepreneur Revolution.

READ THIS BOOK MORE THAN ONCE

I want to encourage you to re-read this book a few times. Some of the ideas hit you the second time around. I know I cover topics quickly and jump from idea to idea. In the second or third read, you will spot something magical. You will click an idea into place and it might just take everything up a notch.

This book contains some powerful ideas. I believe now you're at the end of this book you're ready to perform at a whole new level.

Did you keep an eye out for the new ingredient that must go into everything you do?

I mentioned this ingredient many times in the book but I couldn't say what it is specifically for you. I will leave you to find it.

When you read through this book, did you look for the clues?

The beginning was important, the end is significant but at the centre is where you might find you discover a mountain of value you never noticed when you first looked.

Sometimes people read this book and 'get it'; other times they don't. Some people 'get it' on the second or third read.

I've not hidden this key ingredient from you – if anything it's actually right under your nose.

Whatever you do, don't stop looking. You simply can't build a successful enterprise without this ingredient in the Entrepreneur Revolution.

CASE STUDIES OF 'ENTREPRENEUR REVOLUTIONARIES'

ADÈLE THÈRON

Adèle loves change. Not in the way most people do, as in a holiday or a new outfit. She loves change as a concept; she loves the process of radical transformation.

This love led her to work for several large consulting companies, getting paid megabucks to help large teams of people move on from the shock associated with clashes during mergers, outsourcing or downsizing projects, so they are focused on moving on versus being held back.

Within this corporate sphere, she developed a method for helping people to rapidly transform their lives even after a major setback or turbulent event.

She loved helping people to change and transform but she got frustrated with the structure of the corporate environment.

She felt large companies were missing the humanity of what she was doing. Rather than seeing the radical nature of what's possible for people who go through a changing time, she was being asked to simply tick the boxes in implementing change programmes that were mostly about delivering KPIs versus checking that everyone was emotionally on board.

She decided to set about the task of taking radical transformation to the world. She chose a niche that was close to her heart, helping women who have been through a divorce to recreate their life.

Adèle named her process 'the naked divorce'. She wrote a book on the topic, created products and found partners. She started speaking publicly and soon became a recognised key person of influence in the field.

She constructed an Ascending Transaction Model of products that could be shipped internationally. Soon her business started to attract clients all over the world and partnerships in countries she'd never been to.

She's free to travel, explore and develop herself and her business.

Today she runs a successful global small business and helps men and women all over the world to heal from their divorce. She's taking her methodology and using it to create programmes for other types of emotional trauma. She's still able to consult for corporations and, with her newfound passion, she is able to charge more and do work on her terms.

Adèle let go of the normal corporate work ethos and embraced her passion. She's turned her passion into a business, she delivers massive value and gets well rewarded for it. Adèle is doing what she loves and is already living in the Entrepreneur Revolution.

JEREMY HARBOUR

Jeremy loves deals. He dropped out of school at age 15 to buy and sell goods at a local market. By 18, he'd built a local amusement arcade but, by 20, he went bust and had to start from scratch again.

He did a deal and got started in a telecommunications company. He did some customer deals and it grew. He did lots more deals and he built a large database of clients. He did a partnership deal with a UK membership organisation and ended up with a national business before the age of 30.

At age 34 he did an exit deal and sold his business for a lot of money.

After that he had no reason to work unless he was doing what he loved, which boils down to doing deals.

Today Jeremy lives in Dubai. He advises people on doing deals all over the world.

On a typical day he will be sitting on his 100 ft boat making calls. He's doing deals, floating companies on the stock exchange and advising other people on their deals. He teaches people to buy and sell businesses, he turns around struggling businesses that are in distress, he finds great businesses and gets them the capital they need.

He takes a percentage of the deals he does and makes a small fortune each year based on the success of his deals.

His set-up allows him to travel for about five months of the year without missing a thing. He 'works' a few hours each day from anywhere in the world. In his spare time, he's been able to write books, give talks at conferences and has a global network of deal makers who are trained up on his strategies.

Jeremy isn't stuck in a small business like many people are. He's well aware of the exciting times we live in and he's making the most of it. He's turned his passion for deal making into an exciting business. He's doing what he loves and he's already living in the Entrepreneur Revolution.

PAT LYNES

Pat loves work. He wants the whole world to love it too and champions new ways of working for both individuals and organisations. Pat started his career in interim recruitment, building a division from scratch and turning it into a nine-figure revenue business in just over six years.

But over time he witnessed first-hand how disillusioned most people were becoming with the corporate environment and saw many change initiatives failing amidst a backdrop of burnout and stagnation.

Pat founded Sullivan & Stanley (S&S), an award-winning consultancy disruptor to revolutionise the future of work. S&S is on a mission to help businesses achieve strategic change and innovation in today's rapidly evolving, complex world. It has helped some of the world's leading brands stay ahead of the curve and emerge as trailblazers in their industries.

Pat most recently teamed up with a senior executive from the world of Formula 1 to create a set of guiding principles that big businesses can use to thrive through disruption and drive value at speed to ensure future success. Thousands of senior leaders are applying these lessons every day to make their businesses more successful.

Sullivan & Stanley has become hugely successful and is on an evolution to scale rapidly as Pat shifts his focus to innovation and growth as founder, bringing in a new CEO to lead the team operations. Pat has authored multiple best-selling books on culture, leadership and the future of work. He has also moved his family to an ideal location in Portugal where he runs his business remotely. He isn't just talking about new ways of working, he's living it.

SEB BATES

Seb loves facing challenges head on. In his twenties he learned how to skydive out of planes and then progressed to base jumping off mountains, bridges and cliffs. After a crash landing that almost killed him, he was given the news that he would never walk again.

Considering his income came from teaching martial arts, this news was devastating both personally and professionally. Seb leaned into the pain and hopelessness of the situation and two years later took his first steps again.

He didn't just learn to walk, he also developed his business systems, wrote a book and created his own unique approach to character development for kids.

Today Seb's martial arts school, The Warrior Academy, has locations across the UK and the UAE, he has over 30,000 students and has written two best-selling books.

His focus is using martial arts as a catalyst for developing confidence, conduct and concentration. His martial arts academy teaches lessons about overcoming excess screen usage, avoiding online bullying and keeping a calm mind under pressure.

He has personally taught martial arts to the children of royal families, billionaires and celebrities. His business has become highly profitable, scalable and fun – it is an expression of who he is.

With his father, Seb launched The Bates Foundation and has set up martial arts schools in the economically poorest parts of the world. The schools offer more than martial arts training – they offer important life skills that free students from poverty.

Sebastian is living his life on his terms. He travels the world having adventures, making plenty of profit and making a positive difference in the lives of thousands of families.

SARA MILNE ROWE

Sara loves performance. She started her career as a schoolteacher, helping students to perform at their best. She taught at schools that had a lot of difficult situations going on in the background and created environments where the students could achieve their best.

Sara then trained up in professional coaching skills and launched her company, Coaching Impact. She signed up large organisations as clients and began working with their leadership teams. Sara gathered Olympic athletes, high-ranking military officers and other high-achievers to bring them into the boardrooms of big pharma, banking and tech companies. This unique approach really caught on and her business has grown to become one of the top coaching practices in the UK.

Sara noticed that many high performers overlook the basic building blocks of performance. She wrote a book called *The SHED Method*, which covers sleep, hydration, exercise and diet as fundamentals for success. Her book became widely acclaimed in corporate circles and she has now been able to create digital training resources that are used by thousands of people to better manage their work lives.

Sara never lost her passion for education and has gone back into schools, this time as a high-performance coach, author and entrepreneur. She coaches headteachers and teachers and has created resources for their schools to better equip students for their academic demands.

Sara does all of this while spending a lot of her own time hiking, travelling, and enjoying life. She is a perfect example of achieving high impact while also having a wonderful life outside of business.

JACQUI SHARPLES

Jacqui loves fitness. On most nights of the week you can find her at the athletics field, pole vaulting or sprinting. She believes fitness is what gives people their spark.

Nothing could have illustrated this more than when Jacqui left her corporate job. After years as an engineer in a construction firm she realised that a lot of her colleagues were losing their fitness and losing their will to live.

In a bold move, she quit her high-paying job and got trained up as a fitness trainer. She began delivering fitness training sessions before work in the parks in Melbourne.

After the business started moving, she decided to hone in on a niche and focus her efforts exclusively on corporate women in their 30s.

Jacqui has written a book, created an ATM of products and is now expanding her business with other trainers who want to use her system. In a short space of time, she's become a key person of influence in her field.

She created a specialised programme called 'Love Your Body, Love Your Life' that includes elements of fitness and life coaching to help her clients get fit and reclaim their spark.

She's replaced her high-paid engineering income and now engineers spectacular transformations for her clients along with constructing the life she wants. Jacqui is doing what she loves and is already living in the Entrepreneur Revolution.

To see many examples of people who are transforming their businesses and their lives visit: www.dent.community

ACKNOWLEDGEMENTS

The ideas in this book have come about from many wonderful conversations with important people in my life over the last 20 years.

I would like to sincerely thank:

My parents Andrew and Diane for fostering my entrepreneurial spirit, always encouraging my ideas as well as offering practical support.

My sister Justine for her spark and enthusiasm and friendship.

My wife Aléna who brings out the best in me and has brought so much luck into my life.

My friends and business partners Glen Carlson, Steven Oddy, Donna O'Toole, Lucy McCarraher, Joe Gregory, David Horne and Mike Reid. Long may our adventures continue.

My business mentors who have taken me under their wing over the last 20 years (Jon, Roger, Paul, Mike and others).

The mentor teams on the Dent Global Accelerator Programs – Mike Harris, Nic Rixon, Penny and Thomas Power, Steve Bolton, Ian Elliot, Cathy Burke, Dale Murray CBE, Julia Langkraehr, Matthew Michalewicz, Paul Dunn, Topher Morrison and Kevin Harrington.

Some great entrepreneurial friends who have stimulated my thinking – Jeremy Harbour, Oli Barrett,

Tom Ball, Callum Laing, Mike Carter, Rich Litvin and
Shaa Wasmund.

The awesome people on our team who are building daily
the most dynamic, high-performance entrepreneurial ecosystem. Especially Kristen Schuhen, Donna Antoinette,
Suzy Mudd.

The investors in my businesses who have joined me in taking
the financial risks required to power up a big vision.

My awesome clients who teach me so much about the entrepreneurial journey and who keep my spark burning for
an unfolding Entrepreneur Revolution.

ABOUT DANIEL PRIESTLEY

Daniel Priestley is a successful entrepreneur, international speaker and best-selling author. Daniel started out as an entrepreneur in 2002 (at age 21) and built a multimillion-dollar event marketing and management business before age 25. He has since built several successful businesses in the UK, Australia and USA.

Daniel has bought, sold and turned around businesses in his career as an entrepreneur. He has raised money and built businesses in multiple countries. Daniel has found success in technology, business services, publishing and training. He is fortunate to have been mentored by entrepreneurs who have built multibillion dollar brands.

In 2010, Daniel launched an entrepreneur growth accelerator designed to assist in supporting businesses through three growth phases. Each year, in several cities around the world, Daniel's team selects small businesses to go through the accelerator process. These accelerators have attracted the support of highly celebrated business leaders, investors and companies and are accredited.

In 2020, Daniel co-founded ScoreApp, which is a leading-edge marketing software. It is an AI-enabled tool for businesses to generate warm, data-rich leads using quizzes and assessments.

Daniel Priestley has raised hundreds of thousands of dollars for charity and served as an advisor to key charitable organisations. He is also the best-selling author of *Oversubscribed, 24 Assets* and *Key Person of Influence.*

You can keep in touch with Daniel through Dent Global:

www.dent.global

or on LinkedIn:

www.linkedin.com/in/danielpriestley/

WHAT NEXT?

If you liked this book, please take the time to review it on Amazon.

Daniel Priestley is the author of other entrepreneurship books:

Key Person of Influence
Oversubscribed
24 Assets

BONUS: Send a link or a screenshot of a review or blog post you've written that features this book to us at **reviews@dent.global**, and we will send you a thank you and a complimentary ticket to an event by Daniel's company Dent Global.

To see what's coming up, visit **www.dent.global/events**.

For a preview of Daniel Priestley's *Oversubscribed*, please read on . . .

PRINCIPLE 1: DEMAND AND SUPPLY SET THE PRICE

You likely learned long ago that the market forces of demand and supply determine the price and the profit you'll make. But what you didn't learn is that you can make your own market forces.

The Story of the Two Bidders

I was in a room with 400 people who had come to see renowned entrepreneur and author, Gary Vaynerchuk, share his ideas on social media marketing. He announced at the end of his presentation that he'd be auctioning off a 1-hour one-on-one business consultation with him and the proceeds would go to charity.

He explained that the last time he did a consultation like this he had made several introductions to his network and the person had made an additional $50,000 in less than 30 days. 'It's not just a consultation', he explained, 'It's potentially access to my network – and I know some of the world's most powerful people.'

This had put the audience into a state of frenzy. I opened the auction with a bid of £500 and immediately another person took it to £600. Within a flash the price hit £1000 and the hands kept popping up.

Bids were coming in thick and fast – £2000, £2200, £2400, £2600, £2800.

As the bidding passed the £3000 mark, it came down to two men who clearly both wanted this prize. Everyone else was out of the race, but these two guys kept matching each other and taking the price up another £100 each time.

They were the only two people still bidding in a room with 400 individuals. The rest were sitting patiently or enjoying the spectacle.

The price got up to £3900 with no signs of slowing down. Gary could tell the audience members were getting restless – so he asked the two bidders, 'Will you both pay £4000 each and I will provide a consultation for both of you?'

They agreed, and the hammer went down. Gary had raised £8000 by auctioning off two hours of his time.

I'm not sure how high it would have gone but I do know that it only takes two people to push up the price at an auction. Most of the people in the room didn't bid at all and very few people bid beyond £1500. But that doesn't matter. When the supply is 'one' and there are 'two' who want it, then that price keeps going up. Two people who desire something is enough to oversubscribe the one person who has it. The price keeps going up until one entity gives in.

When Facebook purchased cross-platform mobile messaging app WhatsApp for $19 billion, the number seemed ridiculous to almost everyone on the planet – except one other bidder. Google was the other company who wanted to buy WhatsApp and the two rival companies bid the price into the stratosphere. Had the price been set by a wider market, the general consensus would have been a much lower number.

Too many business owners focus on the entire market place. They are deeply concerned by what the majority will pay rather than finding the small group of people who really value what they offer. But if you focus on the wider market price, you'll always be average.

If Gary Vaynerchuk wanted to try and sell everyone an hour of his time during the auction, he would have probably needed to lower his prices to £200 per hour. And after delivering a month of solid consultations to all 400 people he also would have needed a holiday – and would have had zero energy to write more books or give more talks.

As it turns out, Gary knew that his real value wasn't even the consultation. It was his ability to make a high-level introduction that would be taken seriously because it came from him.

Your value is much higher than you think to a small number of people. You don't need everyone on the planet to see you as in demand; you only need enough people who can drive your price up. Separating from the economy and from your industry requires that you turn your attention to those people who find you highly valuable – and then serve them better than anyone else can.

If two people want your time and only one can get it, your price rises until one of them gives in. Your job isn't to please everyone. Your job is to find those people who can't live without you. So ... who are those people? What is it they want? And where *do you* find them? These questions matter more than the questions that relate to the overall market.

Your price isn't fixed, or set by the overall market. It's a result of being oversubscribed or not.

Let's begin with some basics that I was taught by one of the world's top market traders.

SOME PEOPLE MISS OUT

'Why do markets go up?'

I was sitting in the home office of one of Australia's most successful stock market traders – a man who had traded billions of dollars and who'd been consistently successful trading markets for 20+ years. He was a man for whom people travelled internationally to hear him speak about markets for an hour or two.

I was 22 years old at the time, and I answered him with my best guess: 'Positive news, a good economy, monetary policy, a good CEO; probably they all have an impact, I think.'

'Nice try – but no', he said with a smile, 'Markets go up because there are more buyers than sellers ... and that's it!'

BUYERS   SELLERS

I had forgotten the fundamental truth of economics: the basics of 'demand and supply' that you learn on day one of any economics class. A strong market, a good business plan or a compelling story all help but ultimately your price is set by the balance of supply and demand.

What's more, the market abhors a profit. A profit is only tolerated if demand is higher than supply. No one wants your business to be highly profitable other than its stakeholders. If you tell consumers they can have a cheaper price but the company will lose money and might go out of business, they probably won't even think twice about buying as much as they can. They aren't worried about your profit margins; they are concerned about their own budgets.

This is why you'll only make a profit if you are over-subscribed on your capacity to deliver, and why demand for your stuff must always be greater than your ability to supply it.

People forget the basics. They get caught up in tactics for marketing and lead generation, and they fuss over management styles and team-building techniques, forgetting that all of these activities don't mean much if the business isn't oversubscribed.

The principles set out in this book can be useful across many aspects of your business. For example, if you want to hire top talent, you need to be oversubscribed for top talent. That means that some people need to miss out on the job. If you want impactful publicity you need to be oversubscribed for people who want the story you have to share, so some news outlets won't get the story. If you want to sell products, those products need more buyers than supply can allow for – so again, some people will miss out.

Being oversubscribed requires nothing more than a situation whereby some people who really wanted something had to miss out on having it. Of course, it's a difficult situation because you and your company don't *want* people to miss out. Naturally, you want to sell to everyone who's willing to buy, yet that very mindset prevents you from becoming oversubscribed.

Lots of people want a Ferrari – but the people at Ferrari aren't losing sleep over it. They know that the fact that some people have to miss out is what makes their automobile so coveted. Every product that is oversubscribed has people who didn't get it, even though they were *willing* to buy.

If you can get the balance right and keep yourself oversubscribed – disappointing those people who missed out without them losing interest in you entirely, while still delivering remarkable value to those who got through – you'll have no problems being profitable. If supply is too great and everyone who wants what you have can get what you have, the prices will fall and so will the margins. Eventually your business will make losses.

If you want to be oversubscribed you'll need to get comfortable with some people missing out on what you have to offer. That's how the market works – and that's how it determines your rewards.

PROFITS, LOSSES OR WAGES?

There are three ways the demand and supply equation can play out for your business:

1. **Oversubscribed** – demand is outstripping supply, resulting in profit being tolerated on top of normal wages.
2. **Balanced** – demand and supply are relatively even resulting in normal wages being tolerated but not profit.
3. **Undersubscribed** – excess supply is available above demand, resulting in losses.

It doesn't matter what the product is. The only thing that matters is the relationship between demand and supply. Even when the product stays the same, if that relationship changes, the profitability changes.

In California in the 1980s, millions of people decided that they wanted plastic surgery. The surgeons who could deliver this service were in short supply and they made vast sums of money providing breast enhancements, nose jobs and Botox. Anyone who could perform these operations ended up with a mansion, a yacht, 10 cars and lucrative investments. They were making millions because the market had vastly more buyers than sellers when it came to plastic surgeons.

This is no longer the case nowadays. LA is filled with plastic surgeons. Attracted by the vast available wealth, a whole lot of medical students switched their major in the late 1980s and headed for Beverly Hills to make big money.

But they discovered upon arriving that they weren't the only ones who had this incredible brain wave. By the end of the 1990s the demand and supply relationship returned to a balance and today most plastic surgeons in LA make a normal surgeon's wage.

The plastic surgeons made more money because of a boom that happened across their whole industry. But as you'll see later in this book, it's possible to be completely independent of your industry and build a market of your own. Most people focus on the market that they are in when they think about demand and supply, but in doing so they miss out on an important part of the story. There are cycles in the economy whereby demand from 'consumers' as a whole outstrips supply from 'industry' as a whole. In these times, everyone seems to be doing well and there's an economic boom for almost everyone, such as happened in the era known as the Roaring Twenties.

There are also cycles in your industry whereby demand for *anyone* in a chosen field of work will be outstripped by the available supply. This is known as an industry boom; for example, the dot-com boom in the late 1990s, whereby almost any Silicon Valley company could raise millions for little more than an idea.

It's also possible for businesses and people who play an advanced game to go another layer deep and separate from both the economy and your industry and become a market on your own. You become subject to your own forces of demand and supply independent of anyone else. This is where you can become oversubscribed on your own terms.

The forces of demand and supply work the same when customers and clients see you as separate from your industry. However, you don't need very many people in order to become oversubscribed and to maintain a profitable price if you can get a few key things right.

WILEY END USER LICENCE AGREEMENT

Go to www.wiley.com/go/eula to access Wiley's ebook EULA.

INDEX